THE HOME PET VET GUIDE

CATS

Created and Produced by Martin I. Green

BALLANTINE BOOKS • NEW YORK

THE HOME PET VET GUIDE

CATS

Copyright © 1980 by Martin I. Green
Library of Congress Catalog Card Number: 78-74476
ISBN: 0-345-28945-5

Published in the United States by Ballantine Books, a division of Random House, Inc., New York, and simultaneously in Canada by Random House of Canada, Limited, Toronto, Canada.

This edition published by arrangement with Martin I. Green and Berkshire Studio.

Manufactured in the United States of America
First Edition: APRIL 1980
123456789

CREDITS

Created, Designed & Produced by	MARTIN I. GREEN
Edited by	ROSS FIRESTONE
Research Director	PAUL A. CIRINCIONE
Illustrated by	BOBBI BONGARD
Associate Designer	BOBBI BONGARD
Consulting Veterinarian	DR. HARVEY RHEIN
Editorial Assistant	BERNICE CIRINCIONE
Proofreader	CIA ELKIN
Mechanical Art by	FRANK OSSMANN

Thanks to Leonard Rubin for his invaluable advice and input, and to
Ben Schawinsky and Herbert Sipp for their help and assistance. Thanks, too,
to Michael Albano, Seymour Z. Baum, Martha Donovan, Gail Firestone,
Leslie Kamerling, Janice Lindstrom, Jeff Young and Typographic Concepts.

I am indebted to Nancy Neiman for her ongoing faith and support,
and to Nancy Coffey and Bill Shinker for their enthusiastic participation in
making this book happen.

A very special thanks to Ann Sipp, without whom it would not have been possible.

Finally, to Mary Sipp Green, for her encouragement, understanding and love.

MIG

BERKSHIRE STUDIO PRODUCTION
West Stockbridge, Massachusetts 01266

ACKNOWLEDGMENTS

We wish to thank the following veterinarians for providing us with information
and for reviewing and commenting on the manuscript during its various phases:

William J. Kay, D.V.M.
Chief of Staff
The Animal Medical Center
Speyer Hospital and Caspary Research Institute
New York, New York

Chris Lawson, D.V.M.
The Animal Medical Center
Speyer Hospital and Caspary Research Institute
New York, New York

Andrew Breslin, D.V.M.
Lenox, Massachusetts

For information provided, we would also like to thank:

Patrick Concannon, Ph.D.
New York State College of Veterinary Medicine
Cornell University
Ithaca, New York

Donald Lein, D.V.M., Ph.D.
New York State College of Veterinary Medicine
Cornell University
Ithaca, New York

Thanks, too, to the following for making their facilities available to us and
for their research on our behalf:

Bianca Beary
President
Washington Humane Society
Director of Humane Education, A.S.P.C.A.
Washington, D.C.

Joan Weich
Coordinator of Communications
National Headquarters
American Society for the Prevention of Cruelty to Animals
New York, New York

Jean Rose
Executive Director
The Cat Fanciers' Association
Red Bank, New Jersey

Marna Fogarty
Editor of Cat Fanciers' Association Yearbook
The Cat Fanciers' Association
Red Bank, New Jersey

FOR
MY FRIEND
LEONARD I. AXELRAD,
WHOSE LOVE FOR
ANIMALS, PEOPLE AND LIFE
WILL BE FOREVER INSPIRING

CONTENTS

INTRODUCTION

by Harvey Rhein, D.V.M.

Former President of the Long Island Veterinary Medical Association
Dix Hills Animal Hospital
Huntington, New York

Over the past few decades veterinary medicine has made enormous strides forward. Veterinarians working in private practice, veterinary schools and animal medical centers have developed any number of new and more effective procedures for diagnosing and treating the conditions that beset our pets. Many of the recent advancements in human medicine have also been successfully applied to pet care. As a result, veterinary medicine has now reached a level of sophistication where virtually any type of treatment including brain and cardiac surgery—even the use of pacemakers—is available if required.

Yet for all these advances, many health problems that might have been easily eliminated or prevented continue to persist.

The health of a cat requires the cooperative efforts of both the owner and the veterinarian. And on a day by day basis it is the owner, not the veterinarian, who has to provide the essentials necessary to maintain the cat's good health. The owner must make sure the cat has a nutritious diet, sufficient exercise, adequate grooming and clean, safe living quarters. He must also adhere to the veterinarian's recommendations about inoculations, periodic physical examinations and other routine care. By meeting these responsibilities, the owner should be able to spare his cat many of the painful and debilitating disorders that might otherwise afflict it.

To be sure, even the best preventive care cannot guarantee that the cat won't suffer some illness or injury at some point in its life. When this happens, prompt, effective treatment is often vitally important to minimize the effects and assure a rapid, uncomplicated recovery. Here again, owners play a crucial role, for it falls to them to perceive the symptoms, then either provide the necessary care at home or consult the veterinarian if that is what's required.

Major, even life-threatening problems often arise when owners delay seeking veterinary help because they are not sure something is really wrong or hope that the situation will somehow take care of itself if given enough time. Frequently, a single telephone call could have made the difference. Cat owners should never feel reluctant about calling a veterinarian to discuss the symptoms they have observed in their pets. Veterinarians are busy people, but they much prefer to be distracted by a false alarm than have an illness worsen because the treatment was unnecessarily delayed. By listening to you describe your pet's symptoms and questioning you about them, the veterinarian will probably be able to determine whether you ought to bring the animal in for an examination. He may even be able to guide you to the right treatment without actually having to see the cat. In a very real sense, the owner serves as the cat's voice to the veterinarian. But there is no way for him to bring his training and skills into play if this voice remains silent.

Over the course of my many years as a practicing veterinarian I have come up against such silent voices over and over again, and I think I know why. It certainly isn't because owners don't care about the well-being of their pets. Obviously they do, just as they care about the well-being of all the other members of their households. Rather, it seems to me that the problem is rooted in the fact that so little proper information in a truly useable form has been available to the owners when it was needed.

Through a lack of information I have seen any number of health problems created or compounded by errors in the way cats were housebroken or trained. Any number of times I have seen diseases and other serious conditions allowed to develop because well-intentioned but uninformed owners neglected to give their cats the normal care and maintenance they require. Inadequate diet, pest control, sanitation and immunization may easily lead to illnesses that can seriously impair the cat's health. Perhaps the most dramatic and heart-wrenching example of what can happen from lack of information is when a cat has an accident or other emergency and professional veterinary care isn't immediately available. I have seen countless cases where the owner's best intentions failed to help a pet or even worsened its condition because he didn't know what to do or how to do it.

Up until now, there has been no single comprehensive, concise source of accurate information telling the pet owner what he or she needs to know in easily understandable, nontechnical terms. This book should make up for that deficiency.

The early chapters detail how to prevent health problems from arising in the first place. You will find discussions of such vitally important subjects as nutrition, grooming, housing and sanitation as well as housebreaking and training.

The sections that follow tell you how to cope with the illnesses and emergencies that are most likely to beset your cat. For each illness you will find the major symptoms, the special precautions to be taken and instructions about what has to be done to bring your pet back to health. For each emergency you will find the symptoms that will help you identify what is wrong and step-by-step first-aid procedures to be followed until veterinary aid can be obtained. These procedures are printed in easy to read large type and supported by clarifying illustrations.

To make the information about illnesses and emergencies as accessible as possible, a unique Symptom Recognition Index has also been included. When you notice a particular symptom in your cat, you need only consult this Index to discover what may have caused it. By comparing the symptom you observe in your pet with those described for each of the listed disorders, you should be able to identify the problem, get some sense of its seriousness and find out what to do about it. For emergencies, there is also a special indexing system on the back cover to give you immediate access to the appropriate first aid.

I suggest you begin acquainting yourself with the Symptom Recognition Index as soon as possible and read through the sections on illnesses and emergencies so you will have some familiarity with the recommended procedures before you ever need to use them. You should also keep this book in an accessible place known to everyone in your family.

In my opinion, having this book nearby should do a great deal to put concerned pet owners at ease and make them confident about their ability to deal with almost any health problem that may arise.

PART ONE

A CAT IN THE FAMILY

OF CATS AND MEN

Compared to the dog, which was already part of the human family by early prehistoric times, the relationship between cats and humans is relatively recent, perhaps less than 5,000 years old.

Historical evidence suggests that the Egyptians were the first people to domesticate the cat. One can only guess why this relationship might have begun. Maybe the cats were attracted by the rats and mice that plagued the granaries of ancient Egypt and were given a home when the Egyptians saw how useful they were in ridding the storehouses of these destructive pests. Or perhaps some family of humans found and raised a litter of young cats and discovered them to be lively, intelligent, graceful companions. Whatever the origin, their popularity and importance in Egypt continued to grow, and the animal was ultimately raised to the status of goddess. Great powers were attributed to Pasht, the cat deity, including a special kinship with the moon and the sun. The cat was protected by the full weight of Egyptian law, and it was considered a capital offense to injure one or remove it from the country.

Eventually Phoenician traders, those travelers of the Mediterranean, introduced the cat to the European continent, where its skill at catching rats made it welcome. Centuries later, during the so-called Dark Ages, the same qualities of beauty and mystery that had so deeply impressed the Egyptians were interpreted in an entirely different way by the Christian Church, which proclaimed cats the living incarnation of evil. Cats were burned at the stake, crucified and drowned, and sometimes so were their unfortunate owners. So widespread was this destruction that the delicate balance of nature was seriously upset. It was bad enough that rats and other vermin flourished, but when plague-infested rats accompanied the Crusaders on their return march across Europe, there was nothing to prevent them from infecting the entire continent. By the time Church law changed and the cat had finally reestablished itself in sufficient numbers to combat the problem effectively, millions of humans had died in what was to be remembered as the most lethal epidemic in history.

In time, the cat's usefulness, intelligence and companionability, as well as the qualities of beauty, grace and mystery that had intrigued mankind for so long, fixed the animal firmly in human households all over the world. Cats with the best appearance and temperament were selected over other varieties, and in this way varied breeds possessing unique qualities became established in widespread parts of the world. Continued selective breeding of the best animals produced litters that had still better, more uniform characteristics than their predecessors. Sometimes two different varieties were allowed to breed in the hope that the resulting litter would possess the best qualities of each of its parents. Some of these breeds spread from place to place as their owners explored new territories, fought wars and colonized and traded in foreign countries. Others were closely and jealously guarded by their masters and never seen outside their native regions. Rare and exotic cats were among the most precious gifts exchanged by monarchs.

In our own day, the cat has fit comfortably into every setting where human beings are to be found. It is at home in high-rise apartments and accommodates itself admirably to traveling by car and jet plane. And while it still serves its traditional function of catching mice and rats, it has become increasingly valued for its companionship as a family pet. Given its inborn virtues and ability to adapt to new circumstances and demands, it seems likely that the relationship between cats and humans will only continue to prosper and grow.

THE DECISION TO GET A CAT

It has not been one relationship, of course, but millions of separate and distinct ones all differing from one another, each taking its particular form from the multiple interplay of individual cat, person, need and circumstance.

Still, several common reasons are usually involved, either singly or in combination, in the decision to get a cat:

• The single most popular reason is for the companionship it provides. By nature, cats are almost ideal companions. They are excellent judges of mood and rarely impose their presence when you wish to be left alone. Yet they are also highly affectionate creatures and love to be stroked, showing their pleasure by the throaty purring that is the unmistakable sign of feline contentment. Cats are endlessly entertaining to watch as they groom themselves or play or snoop about indulging their legendary curiosity, always attentive to every sound and movement. And unlike dogs, they are inherently clean, easily housebroken and do not have to be walked. Cats adjust to any household, whatever its activity level. They make excellent pets for adult couples and families with children, and people who live alone find that they can brighten an otherwise lonely existence.

• Some people decide to get purebred cats so they can breed them. This is a more costly and demanding undertaking than a novice might suppose. Most inexperienced owners who breed their pets actually lose money. It doesn't usually become profitable until done on a larger, more efficient basis.

• Few owners get their cats specifically so they can enter them in cat shows, but many people ultimately do find this an interesting and challenging hobby. Preparing the cat to compete is not a simple matter. It requires months of grooming and considerable cost. But if the cat does well in the competition it is awarded points that are applied toward championship status, and in addition to the satisfaction that comes with raising a champion, the cat's value for breeding purposes is also increased significantly. This is why professional breeders are especially interested in having their cats do well in shows.

Adding a cat to the family can be pleasurable, exciting, challenging and even educational, but these benefits do not come without cost, effort and increased responsibility. You would do well to keep this fact in mind before making a final decision to bring a cat into your home. Every year a significant percentage of new pets are sold, given away, abandoned and even destroyed by families that have changed their minds for one reason or another. Some of these reasons have to do with the cat itself. It may develop the annoying habit of spraying furniture or turn out to be destructive or vicious without provocation. Other reasons have more to do with the owner's inability or disinclination to provide the care and attention the cat requires. Sometimes problems develop that could not have been anticipated. You might not know someone in your family is allergic to cat hair. But, unfortunately, the problems are all too often entirely predictable.

Prospective owners must carefully and honestly consider whether they and the other members of their household are truly prepared for the extra work and effort that necessarily come with a cat. It must be fed once or twice a day, kept in good health—the responsibilities are considerable. And they continue seven days a week, 52 weeks a year.

If you are considering getting a cat for your children to "teach them responsibility" or because they desperately want one, you should make sure they are old enough to treat it properly. If your youngsters aren't yet sufficiently mature to understand that a cat has feelings like all other living beings and may not tolerate being chased, shouted at, teased or hurt, it would be better to postpone the gift until they are older.

The point is, if there are good reasons to suspect that a cat would not fit into your home right now, do not get one. Wait until the time is more opportune. Then, if and when you do decide to add a cat to your family, the experience is much more likely to be pleasurable for all the parties involved in the relationship —you, your family and the cat itself.

SELECTING THE RIGHT CAT

Once you have decided to get a cat, you are still left with the question of what sort of cat to get. Will it be a kitten or a fully grown animal? A male or a female? Long-haired or short? Purebred or mixed breed? If a purebred, which one? There are dozens to choose from. If you are considering a mixed breed, the decision isn't any easier. They come in a virtually unlimited number of combinations. Unless you already have your heart set on a particular animal, the whole matter can be terribly confusing.

It will help clarify your thinking if you first ask yourself what purpose you want the cat to serve. Do you want a family pet? A show cat? A purebred you can breed? A certain kind of cat may be well-suited to some of these purposes but not to others. It will also help to keep in mind practical considerations shaped by the specific circumstances of your life. If you're concerned about hairs all over your newly upholstered furniture, remember that long-haired cats do shed more than shorthairs. Obviously, it makes sense to fit the givens that come with certain cats with the givens of your own situation.

Although there are often significant differences between cats of the same breed and even between members of the same litter, experience suggests that there are some reliable generalizations that may help guide you toward the best cat for your purposes. Male cats, for example, tend to be more aggressive than females. Spayed females usually have the fewest health problems and are better around young children. Because your cat will be an integral part of your family, you must have a realistic sense of the pros and cons of each option before coming to a final choice.

PUREBRED OR MIXED BREED?

Whether you select a purebred or a mixed breed will be influenced by your personal preference, budget and the future plans you have for the cat. Purebreds have some value for breeding purposes. Mixed breeds do not. Purebreds can participate in cat shows for championship status. Mixed breeds cannot. Neither choice, however, assures you of a healthier, smarter or more lovable pet.

As the name suggests, a purebred is a cat whose predecessors for many generations have all come from the same breed. Although there are millions of them in this country, they represent only a small minority of all cats.

Purebreds are initially more costly than mixed breeds but do not usually cost more to feed and maintain. The higher initial cost is due in part to stud fees, veterinary care before and after whelping and the other expenses the breeder incurs to produce a salable kitten. As might be expected, kittens from championship bloodlines or from rare and unusual breeds are the most expensive of all purebreds.

Perhaps the main advantage of purebreds is that so much is known about them. Owners, breeders, veterinarians and others with a special interest in a breed have observed and written about all the specific characteristics that have been passed down through the generations, and this information is widely available to anyone who cares to seek it out. If you are considering a particular breed, you can easily find out about such things as the expected thickness and color of the fur, the cat's size and structure, its special problems and even its temperament and personality. With some of the older breeds, such observations may have been accrued over the course of hundreds or even thousands of years. The availability of such detailed information has also made it possible for these cats to be improved through systematic selective breeding that emphasizes their best qualities and reduces or eliminates their hereditary faults. The end result is to give the prospective buyer the best possible basis for making an informed decision by doing away with much of the guesswork involved in predicting the qualities a kitten will have when it matures. The section on **THE BREEDS OF CATS** gives you a good distillation of what you may expect to find in the most popular breeds available in this country.

Keep in mind, however, the fact that a cat is a purebred does not necessarily assure you of quality. Before making a purchase, you must always evaluate the particular cat you are considering as well as the reputation of the breeder. Poor quality purebreds often result from indiscriminate or irresponsible breeding practices, such as mating two cats from the same litter. Typically, such practices follow close behind a sudden increased demand for a particular breed because of the interest generated by a movie, book or news story. Efforts to produce more cats quickly to satisfy this demand may result in litters with poor characteristics or hereditary defects.

If you are thinking about buying a purebred, make a point of becoming somewhat familiar with the "standards" or ideal characteristics of that breed. One of the main factors determining the price you will have to pay is the extent to which a given cat fits these standards. You might find it both enjoyable and informative to learn about the breed at first hand by attending a cat show. You will be able to watch how each breed is judged, talk to some of the owners and breeders in your area and discover the qualities that may lead you to or away from a particular breed. Keep in mind, though, that owners and others with a special commitment to one kind of purebred may not offer very much information about its limitations or shortcomings.

The overwhelming majority of cats are mixed breeds. This means that their characteristics are more a product of genetic luck than of carefully planned selective breeding. It is, therefore, much more difficult to predict what the appearance and temperament of a mixed breed kitten will be when it matures. Even kittens from the same litter may vary widely from each other and from their parents. Each kitten is a truly unique individual, different from all others in the world.

There are exceptions, but mixing of the breeds usually produces sturdy, intelligent offspring that possess the best qualities of their predecessors. They are also much less likely to embody hereditary defects than purebreds are.

KITTEN OR MATURE CAT?

Should you be thinking about a kitten, remember that it will require more time, care and patience than a mature cat. It will have to be fed more frequently and also be housebroken. Moreover, a kitten does not have the resistance and strength of an older cat, so an illness may have much more serious consequences.

The extra effort is certainly not without its compensations. A kitten is one of the most adorable babies in the animal world and provides endless pleasure and enjoyment to everyone around it. Most kittens learn quickly and adjust easily to other pets and all the other aspects of a new home. Understandably, if you raise a kitten to maturity, it will be closer to you and the other members of your family than a newly arrived mature cat could ever be.

The age at which the kitten is adopted is crucially important. Newborn kittens are wonderfully appealing, but they shouldn't be separated from the mother too early, certainly not before they have completed nursing and no longer require her milk. The ideal age for adoption ranges from about six or eight weeks to around four months. Kittens older than four months may have already begun to pick up bad habits from littermates and adult cats, which may be too late to change. If the kitten has been pretty much isolated from human contact for these first four months, it will probably not make a suitable pet. For some reason, such cats fail to form strong attachments to human beings. These animals tend to run away over and over again and seldom return home by choice.

For some people, fully grown cats offer certain important advantages. They are stronger, better able to take care of themselves and much less susceptible to illness. Since they are likely to have been already immunized and neutered, they also save their new owners the cost of these early medical expenses. Mature cats only need to be fed once or twice a day and usually need less sustained attention than kittens. Nor do they need to be housebroken. When a fully grown cat is brought into a new home and subjected to a new routine, it may make an occasional mistake, but this period of uncertainty usually passes quickly. Although it does take more time for a mature cat to adjust to new surroundings, especially if there are other pets in the house, by and large it is probably a better choice if you don't have the time, energy or inclination to deal with the not inconsiderable needs of a kitten.

The single most important personal quality in a cat is probably its personality. Since you have not raised the mature cat from the outset and are getting the product of someone else's efforts, you must be sure it has the qualities of temperament you want or at least does not have the qualities that you don't want. It is usually far easier to judge a fully grown cat's disposition than a kitten's, and you can be reasonably sure that its personality will remain pretty much the same after you take it home with you. Adult personality is exceedingly difficult to predict in a kitten even when the parents are known, especially if it is a mixed breed. Only time will tell how it will turn out.

Still, it takes a fair amount of observation and judgment to determine what a mature cat is really like. What its present owners tell you has only limited value. For one thing, their judgment of the cat's disposition may simply be wrong. They may believe, for example, that because the cat has never bitten or scratched anyone it hasn't an aggressive bone in its body, when the fact is any cat will scratch and bite if sufficiently provoked or placed under high enough stress. For another thing, the present owners' evaluation is necessarily based upon their experience with the animal in their own environment, and your household may be very different. If the cat has only known a tranquil existence among considerate adults, it may exhibit a radically different personality when taken to a home full of noisy, rambunctious children. Changes from one sort of household to another may bring out problems that never existed before (as well as put an end to problems that previously seemed insoluble). Particularly if your home differs from the sort of place it grew up in, you ought to spend considerable time observing how the cat reacts to various situations before you decide to adopt it.

MALE OR FEMALE?

Both male and female cats make excellent pets, and either one is a good choice. In the most general sense, females are likely to be more cautious, gentle and quiet. Spayed females are commonly held to be the most pleasant cats with the nicest dispositions and fewest undesirable traits. Males tend to be somewhat larger than females as well as more friendly, lively and vigorous. They are also much more likely to roam and get into fights with other cats, particularly other males.

Older cats tend to develop physical problems that are characteristic of their gender. As they age, some females develop urinary conditions that cause them to lose control of their urine. If unspayed, they are also prone to uterine infections and ovarian, uterine and breast cancer. Males may develop crystals in their urinary system and have other urinary problems. Some of these conditions can be alleviated with prescription drugs. Others may require surgery, sustained treatment or ongoing care at home. The point is that neither males nor females are necessarily healthier or less subject to illness.

Obviously, a female is preferable if you look forward to having kittens around your home.

LONG-HAIRED OR SHORT?

If you are considering a long-haired cat, be aware that those beautiful showy coats do shed and do require substantial care and grooming. To maintain the cat's appearance and keep its hair from becoming knotted and matted, you will have to brush and comb it at least once a day. Matting is a serious problem and can only be prevented by continuous attention. Regular brushing is also necessary to control the amount of loose hair the cat leaves deposited on floors, furniture and clothing as well as to minimize what it can swallow when it grooms itself. If this hair forms into hair balls in the cat's intestines, the animal can become dangerously ill. All cats are subject to the problem, but it is most common in long-hairs. Keep in mind that some long-haired breeds shed more than others and that large long-haired cats tend to leave more loose hairs around than small ones do.

Should you decide on a long-haired pet, you will also routinely have to clean the area under the tail to prevent the formation of packs of matted hair. Unless cleaned away promptly, they can obstruct the cat's normal bowel functions and lead to painful irritation, inflammation and infection. Particularly when the cat gets older, flies may be attracted to this area in hot weather and seriously threaten the animal's health by depositing maggots in its flesh.

Short-haired cats also require regular grooming, of course, but not nearly as much.

WHERE TO GET YOUR CAT

There are so many mixed breed kittens and cats looking for homes that you should have no trouble finding one that suits you perfectly if you are willing to look around a bit.

Mention to your friends and neighbors that you want a cat, and it probably won't be long before someone with a new litter offers you one.

You can also check your neighborhood bulletin boards and the classified section of your local newspaper. They are usually filled with ads offering to give away kittens at no cost to good homes.

Your local Society for the Prevention of Cruelty to Animals (SPCA) and Humane Society Shelter probably have large numbers of mixed breeds available for immediate adoption. Should you select one of these animals, you are likely to be saving it from an early, if painless, death. With luck, you may even find some purebreds waiting for homes.

Pet shops are another good traditional source for cats. Many offer both mixed breeds and purebreds, though they tend to sell only the breeds that are in greatest demand. If you have a more unusual sort of cat in mind, the store may not be able to get it for you right away.

Purebreds can also be obtained from amateur and commercial breeders. Keep in mind that the quality and cost of purebreds vary widely and do not necessarily have a direct relationship to each other. Some breeders are seriously dedicated to offering only fine examples of a breed that are free from hereditary defects and temperamentally well-suited to modern family life. Others are more concerned with selling quantity than quality. Be particularly wary if the breed you are considering has become highly popular within the last year or two.

If it is at all possible, check the reputation of a pet shop or breeder with owners who have gotten their pets there. What they tell you should give you a pretty good idea of what to expect. In the final analysis, of course, the responsibility for selecting the pet falls to you and the other members of your family.

CHECKING THE CAT OUT

The cat you choose is going to be yours for some years to come, so take the time to look at a number of pets before making your final decision. If it turns out that the first cat you saw is ultimately the one you like best, you can always go back for it. It is usually better to take the chance it might be gone than to select impulsively the first nice animal you see. Even if you have had no previous experience judging cats, the process of looking around and comparing will help sharpen your judgment.

When you have narrowed your choice down to a particular cat, spend a few minutes observing its appearance and behavior to make sure it is in good health. Of all the factors to keep in mind when coming to your final selection, this is the single most important.

• A healthy cat is active, alert, curious, responsive and able to move about freely without hesitation. It should not seem unusually shy, frightened or dejected.

• The body should be muscular and firm without a potbelly or wobbly back legs.

• When you run your hands over the cat's chest, you should be able to feel the ribs but not be able to stick your fingers between them.

• The animal ought to be relatively clean. A healthy cat is able to care for itself; a sick cat is not.

• The fur should be smooth, thick and glossy, with no bare or bald spots.

• Check the skin underneath. It should be clean and have a healthy pink color, without lumps, redness, scales, dryness or evidence of fleas.

• Make sure there are no symptoms of respiratory illness such as sneezing, coughing, wheezing, discharges from the eyes or nose, or debris around the lips or mouth.

• Signs of diarrhea around the cat's tail may also indicate illness. The anus should not look swollen or protrude.

• Examine the inside of the cat's ears to make sure they are clean and free of soil-like material, wax, scabs and the like.

• Check the inside of the mouth. The teeth should be white; the gums pink, firm and without sores or angry red areas.

• There are exceptions, but keep in mind that white cats with blue eyes are often totally deaf and those with one blue eye and one of another color may be deaf in one ear. To check the cat's hearing, call to it while it is turned away from you and observe if it responds to your voice.

• If you are looking at a kitten, check the conditions in and around the litter as well as the appearance of its littermates. They should tell you something about how well it has been cared for. As a general rule, the less contact a kitten has had with other cats and dogs, the better its chances of being free of infectious diseases and parasites. Find out from the seller whether it has been wormed and inoculated or if this will be your responsibility.

Final confirmation that the cat is healthy should come from a veterinarian. Plan to have it examined within three or four days after you bring it home. Make sure it can be returned to the seller within some reasonable period, say ten days to two weeks, if the vet finds it in poor health or unacceptable for any other reason. Most responsible pet dealers are willing to agree to this sort of conditional sale. The incubation period for many infectious diseases is between a week and ten days, and the symptoms may not become apparent before then.

Almost equally as important as the cat's health is its disposition. It is extremely difficult to make accurate predictions about a cat's personality if you haven't been able to observe it over a long period of time in a wide variety of circumstances. Even then, owners who have had their pets for years are often startled by the personality changes that can be produced by particularly stressful situations. The changes that take place in a kitten as it matures can be especially dramatic. Still, by spending a few minutes carefully watching how the cat reacts, you will have a fairly sound basis for deciding whether or not it is temperamentally suited to you.

With the seller's permission, take the cat out of the sight of its littermates. Place it down on the floor, walk a few steps away, then drop down, offer the cat your hand and call to it. Notice the way it responds. Also observe its reactions when you try to pet, handle and restrain it. Does it welcome your hand? Does it struggle? Does it run away from you? How does it react when you walk away as if you were leaving?

THE FIRST DAYS AT HOME

You should begin to make preparations for your new pet even before you bring it home:

• Unless you have chosen a mature, well-trained animal that can be trusted anywhere in the home, it will be necessary to set aside an area where the new arrival can be confined safely and comfortably. A small warm room with few furnishings and an easily cleaned tile floor would be just about ideal.

• Do everything you can to make the room as safe as possible for the cat. For example, electrical wires that might be chewed should be removed or hidden out of reach. The same should be done with toxic chemicals, glassware and small objects that could be swallowed. Remember that a cat is a curious animal and may climb up on furniture to get to something it finds particularly interesting.

• If the cat isn't yet housebroken, cover the entire floor with several thicknesses of newspaper.

• Place the cat's bed in the room. Also put in a few toys—a hard ball with a rattle, a catnip ball or mouse, etc.

The cat's arrival at your home is an understandably exciting event, especially if you have children. Still, you must make every effort to keep things as subdued as possible. Keep in mind that your new pet is in the midst of an unusually stressful period of change. It has just been separated from its previous owner or its mother and littermates, and every aspect of its usual routine has been disturbed. What happens over the next few weeks will influence how it feels in its new home for years to come.

The cat will need at least a few days to explore its new surroundings and gradually adjust to them. Until it understands that you mean it no harm and will provide food, water, shelter and companionship, it is bound to feel a fair amount of uncertainty. If you have another cat or a dog, it might be wise to keep it elsewhere in the house until the new arrival has had a chance to begin its adjustment. After a few days, the two animals can be allowed to meet under your supervision.

During this period, patience and gentle handling are among the most important things you can provide. Make sure that everyone, especially the children, understands that loud noises, heavy hands and sudden movements can frighten the cat and prolong the adjustment period. Children under about six years old should be closely supervised when they are around the pet. Particularly if it is a young kitten, they may unintentionally injure it. You may notice that while the cat is still gaining confidence and adjusting to its new surroundings, it may not purr or be at all playful. This

sort of mild withdrawal is fairly common and no cause for concern unless accompanied by other symptoms of illness. As the adjustment period proceeds, the cat will perk up and become its normal playful self.

The first day is usually the most difficult. Place the cat in the area you have prepared for it, and give it a bowl of water and a small amount of food such as cooked hamburger or semi-moist cat food. Don't be surprised if it isn't hungry.

If you are very fortunate, the cat will be so tired out by all the excitement of the first day that it will fall into a sound sleep and not awaken until the next morning. A more realistic expectation is that it will probably cry and carry on for most, maybe all, of the night.

If you have a kitten, you may be able to make it feel secure enough to sleep by simulating a littermate out of a hot water bottle filled with warm water and wrapped in a towel. This has the best chance of working if you place the towel in the litter of kittens to get their scent on it before you bring your new pet home. A loudly ticking alarm clock or a radio tuned in to an all-night talk show might also do the job. Every situation is different and requires a somewhat different approach, so experiment a bit to find the method that works best for you. And though it may be difficult, try to keep your patience and hold on to your temper. Within a few nights, the cat will settle down and everyone will be able to sleep peacefully once again.

Even if care of the cat will ultimately be your child's responsibility, these early weeks are too important to getting the cat off to a good start to be left exclusively to a child. The youngster may be able to feed the animal perfectly well, but children usually do not understand all the complexities of housebreaking, handling and training. Your child can certainly help, but it is far better for everyone, including the cat, if it is supervised and trained by an adult. Housebreaking should be started immediately to ensure the fastest possible development of good behavior patterns. The training will only be harder to accomplish if it is deferred for these crucial first weeks and the cat begins to settle into habits you find unacceptable.

SELECTING A VETERINARIAN

At about the same time you decide to get a cat, begin looking for the veterinarian who will provide the health services it will periodically require throughout its life. These services range from routine examination and preventive care to treatment of acute illnesses and life-threatening emergencies. The three main factors to consider in making your choice are professional competence, the facilities and equipment available for diagnosis and treatment and the attitudes and personality of the veterinarian as they may affect your relationship.

The practice of veterinary medicine is restricted to men and women who have been graduated from an accredited school of veterinary medicine and met the state licensing requirements. Beyond that, competence can vary widely, just as it does in all the other healing arts.

Unless you are already familiar with a veterinarian from an earlier pet, begin by asking cat owners you know for the names of veterinarians they would recommend. Try to determine the kind of care their cats required and what their experience has been. Predictably, most owners will have only good things to say about their vets, so it might be valuable to ask if they have switched veterinarians recently and, if so, why. Keep questioning friends and relatives until you have a list of three or four veterinarians who have been enthusiastically recommended by their clients. As an alternative, you can consult your telephone directory or the veterinary medical association in your area for the names of local practitioners.

Beginning at the top of your list, call the veterinarian's office and request information about the fee structure and the facilities and services available. They can vary widely from one vet to the next. You should be able to get this information about such basic matters as routine examinations, inoculations and neutering.

Armed with as much preliminary information as you can gather, call the veterinarian back and introduce yourself to him. Indicate that you are about to buy a cat and are telephoning at the recommendation of one of his clients. Tell him you would like to meet him personally and tour his facilities if that's at all possible. Veterinarians have busy schedules, but they will usually oblige this sort of request.

When you meet the vet face to face you will begin to form some preliminary impressions about what a professional relationship with him might be like. What you are seeking is an individual who inspires confidence in his skills, seems to have sincere concern and compassion for his patients and shows sensitivity to your feelings as a pet owner.

As you look around the facilities, notice whether the examination and treatment areas seem clean and well-equipped. Do the patients look well cared for and reasonably content? Are healthy animals kept separated from sick ones? If boarding is available, are the housing and exercise facilities adequate? You might also tell the vet about the type of cat you are considering and ask him for his opinion about your choice.

In all likelihood, this brief meeting is the only direct basis you will have for deciding whether or not you want your cat treated by this person. Have confidence in your feelings and judgment. They are probably correct. If for any reason you come away with a negative impression, move on to the next veterinarian on your list.

THE FIRST TRIP TO THE VETERINARIAN

If your new cat seems healthy, it is usually best to wait three or four days before taking it to its first visit to the veterinarian. Your observations about how it behaves at home before then can provide the vet with a good bit of important information. Does it have a good appetite? Do its bowels and bladder seem to function normally? Does it walk, run, play and appear to be enjoying itself? Have you noticed any symptoms of illness?

Take along a specimen of the cat's stool in a closed container. The veterinarian will perform a routine analysis and, if necessary, treat the animal for internal parasites. Also bring a record of any vaccinations the cat may have already had.

A kitten should see the vet when it is about six or eight weeks old. If this is the first visit, the veterinarian will take the cat's health history and give it a general examination. He will also give it the first in a series of immunizations that will protect it from several serious illnesses. Unvaccinated kittens are particularly susceptible to illnesses and are poorly prepared to survive them. The incubation period for certain illnesses is ten days or longer, so the symptoms may not appear until after the vet has examined the kitten and found it in good health. Should this happen, inform the veterinarian immediately, as well as the cat's previous owner.

ENVIRONMENT

THE OUTDOOR CAT

If you live in the country or suburbs and have a yard or other open space, you may want your cat to spend much of its time outside the house. Cats like the outdoors. They enjoy the opportunity it gives them for exercise, exploration and adventure. To determine how much time your pet ought to spend there, you will have to take into account the climate and its particular physical characteristics.

Some cats enjoy being outdoors even in cold weather. Others were never intended by nature to endure the cold or have lost some of nature's protection from the elements through generations of selective breeding and domestication. Such animals are much more comfortable sharing man's increasingly indoor style of life. Most cats, though, are quite content to spend some or even all the daylight hours outside the house if they can come inside for companionship in the evening and aren't forced to endure the discomforts of snow or rain.

There are, however, a number of precautions to take before letting a new cat outside the house by itself:

• Because of their susceptibility to illness, kittens should be at least three months old before they are permitted outside.

• To give a new cat time to adjust, outdoor periods should be short at first, then gradually lengthened over the next week or two. Particularly in a young cat, sudden exposure to extremes of temperature can result in serious illness.

• Teach your cat its name and to come when you call. A cat will learn its name easily if you repeat it often as you feed and pet it. If you make a point of blowing a whistle or ringing a bell to call it to eat, after awhile it will come to you whenever it hears these sounds.

• Your pet should have received its first series of vaccinations before coming into contact with other cats outside the home.

• Cats have a way of straying, so make sure your pet has a tag on its collar giving your name and telephone number in case it gets lost or becomes injured far from home.

• To prevent unwanted litters, you might also consider having your cat altered before permitting it to roam.

Especially if you let your cat go out unsupervised, you should make adequate provisions for its safety, health and comfort. One very important thing you can do is restrict it to a particular area rather than turn it loose to roam at will. Keeping the cat on your own property is not only a matter of law in many communities but obvious good sense. It will keep your pet from becoming a real or imagined nuisance to the neighbors, limit the mischief it can become involved in and, most importantly, protect it from automobiles, the single greatest threat to its life.

An enclosed yard will confine a dog quite adequately but won't really work with a cat. The animal will simply climb out. A much better solution, especially if the cat is to live outdoors, is to set aside an area exclusively for your pet's use and enclose it around the sides and top with metal mesh or chain link fencing. Keeping the cat out of reach will prevent it from fighting with other animals in the neighborhood and make it more difficult for it to catch and eat small game, which often carry parasites and infectious diseases.

The enclosure should be large enough to allow the cat to run around and play without being cramped. If possible, the area should be partially shaded throughout the day and near a convenient source of water. Whenever you place the cat inside the enclosure, put its litter tray in with it. If the cat spends a considerable amount of time outside every day, you should provide it with some sort of comfortable, well-insulated, weatherproof shelter. Also keep close watch on the cat to make sure it stays in good health. Because outdoor cats are not as much under their owners' eyes as indoor cats, health problems are less likely to be noticed until they become quite serious. Keep in mind that outdoor cats are especially prone to fleas, ticks and other parasites. And to emphasize an earlier point, if left to run loose, they may also be hit by cars and get into fights with dogs and other cats as well as porcupines, skunks and other wild animals.

Cats are born hunters, and there is very little you can do to stop them from chasing birds and small animals. Even when well fed, they continue to stalk their natural prey for sport. If you wish, you can tie a bell on your pet's collar, but a cat moves with such stealth that it may not sound a warning until it is too late. Trimming the cat's nails too short or removing them entirely will not change its behavior, only leave it less able to climb and defend itself from its enemies. The only time declawing is appropriate is when a cat is so vicious or destructive that there is no other alternative short of getting rid of it.

In cold weather, an outdoor cat may seek shelter under a parked automobile or even climb up inside the motor compartment to warm itself on the engine. If you should start up your automobile before the cat has a chance to get away, it can be seriously injured or killed. To prevent this from happening, blow your horn, then wait a few seconds before you turn on the ignition and drive off.

THE INDOOR CAT

Cats adapt quite well to a completely indoor life and are happy to be in more or less constant contact with people. There are, however, a number of things you can do to ensure the animal's well-being:

• The cat's natural tendency to explore and climb may give it all the exercise it needs even within the limited confines of a small apartment. But continuous confinement without regular exercise is extremely bad for its health because neither the appetite nor the circulatory system is being properly stimulated. Pets kept in this condition are likely to become obese and old before their time. If you find your cat digging into furniture or drapes, it probably isn't being exercised adequately. Cats usually scratch this way to stretch their bodies and clean and sharpen their nails. A wooden scratching post will give the cat the exercise it requires and save your living room as well. Posts covered with coarse fabric or carpeting can painfully snag the cat's nails and may cause the animal to lose a nail if it becomes frightened and tries to pull itself free. The scratching post will also allow the cat to satisfy its urge to dig and scratch. Special mats are also made for this purpose.

• An indoor cat's nails should be trimmed regularly so they don't become too long. You can have your veterinarian do it for you or do it yourself; see **NAILS,** page 32.

• A house cat should always have its own special area. Select a spot that is comfortably warm and easy to keep clean. Clear it of rugs and other furnishings that may become spoiled if the cat has an accident or becomes ill. Furnish it with the cat's bed and a few toys so it can be comfortable and content.

• If you house the cat in a basement or garage, cover its space with a mat, blanket or section of old carpet to protect it from the concrete floor. Cats that spend extended periods in direct contact with concrete tend to develop arthritis at a relatively early age. It is not unusual for cats to seek out the coolness of concrete in warm weather, but this should be discouraged in older and arthritic animals.

• Make sure the cat gets enough human contact to keep it friendly and socialized. Cats kept isolated for long periods may develop behavior problems and grow less reliable as house pets, particulary with the children in the family.

LIVING QUARTERS

A cat can find a comfortable place to sleep almost anywhere, but it should be given its own sleeping quarters.

If your cat sleeps indoors, it will probably feel most safe and secure sleeping in the area you have chosen as its special place. Select a warm, quiet spot for its bed, well away from heavy household noise and activity. A great variety of cat beds are available at pet shops, or you can make one yourself. A heavy three-sided cardboard box or carton will do nicely as long as it is large enough to keep the cat from feeling cramped. Line the bottom with a pillow or soft pad protected with several layers of washable covers. To minimize cold drafts and dampness, elevate the bed several inches above the floor.

Cats aren't really well-suited to a completely outdoor life, particularly in cold weather. Most owners bring their pets into the house at night or give them

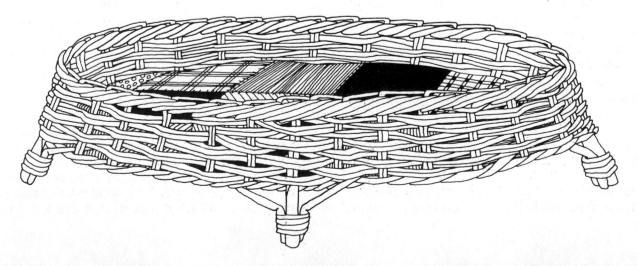

shelter in a garage or barn. A cat that does stay out-doors will require a sturdy, well-insulated, draft-free shelter to protect it from wind, cold and rain. You can purchase a cat shelter or construct one yourself. Plans for various types of shelters can be found in the public library or in the numerous magazines published for the weekend handyman.

Here are some important points to keep in mind when buying or building the cat's shelter:

- It should be made entirely of waterproof materials suitable for outdoor use.
- All paints must be lead-free and nontoxic.
- The shelter will be easier to keep clean if the roof is removable or hinged to permit full access to the interior.
- There should be a small entry area that separates and protects the main interior space from the outside weather.
- To block out wind and rain, the entrance and the opening between the entry area and main space ought to be curtained with canvas or some other heavy cloth. The curtains should be slightly wider than the entrance-ways and hung so that air can circulate freely and the cat doesn't have any difficulty getting in and out.
- The entire structure ought to be elevated four or five inches above the ground.

The shelter should be placed somewhere within the same fenced-in area you have chosen for the cat to play in, in a spot protected from cold winds. If possible, face the doorway away from the north wind. Since the ideal location may be different in summer than winter, it ought to be possible to move the structure as the seasons change.

Pad the floor of the shelter with a blanket, rug or other soft material so the cat will be able to sleep in comfort. Remember to wash the bedding regularly.

Decide where you want the cat to eat and drink, and make sure this spot is always accessible to the animal. If you feed the cat outdoors, make certain the area is protected from sun and rain as well as from ants and other pests that might be attracted to the food.

Food and water should be placed near each other. The water bowl ought to be heavy and stable enough to keep the cat from tipping it over. Inexpensive bowls with weighted bottoms are available in almost any pet shop. For the cat's food, use a shallow dish or pan rather than a bowl so your pet won't have to use its paws to get the food out of the bottom. It will make clean up easier indoors if you put several thicknesses of news-paper under the containers. Make a point of changing the paper frequently.

SANITATION AND HYGIENE

Your cat will need a litter tray for its toilet functions. You will be able to find a suitable one at any pet supply store.

- Make sure the tray is made of non-porous material such as plastic, stainless steel or baked enamel, so it will be easy to clean and resistant to corrosion from the cat's urine.
- It should be about 4 to 6 inches deep and large enough to keep the cat from showering the floor with litter material when it covers up its wastes.
- Fill the pan with 2 to 3 inches of sand, sawdust, shredded newspaper or commercial cat litter.
- Remember that the cat must step into the pan to use it, so keep the animal off counter tops and tables where food is prepared and served.
- Litter material should be changed every 3 or 4 days (shredded newspapers more often) and the pan washed with soap and water. The life of the litter material can be extended somewhat by removing the solid waste every day with a scoop or sieve.
- A half cup of baking soda mixed with the litter will help keep the tray free of unpleasant odors. If the tray is maintained properly, odor shouldn't really be a problem.
- Clean the pan monthly with disinfectant. Make sure to give it a good rinsing to remove all traces of the chemicals.
- To protect your personal health, wash your hands

thoroughly after handling or changing the pan.

Pregnant women should not handle the pan at all or do so only with the greatest concern for their per-sonal cleanliness. This caution is necessary because of the danger of toxoplasmosis, a parasitic disease that can be spread to humans through direct contact with the feces of an infected cat. Should the expectant mother become infected, the disease can cause perma-nent brain damage to her unborn children. If no one else is around to take charge of the litter tray, then the risk can be all but eliminated by cleaning the tray thoroughly every day. The parasite eggs present in the feces of the infected cat must incubate for several days before they become capable of spreading the disease. The expectant mother should always wear rubber gloves during the cleaning and wash her hands carefully when she is done. If any woman in the house-hold becomes pregnant or plans to become pregnant, it is a good idea to have your veterinarian give the cat a blood test to determine if it has toxoplasmosis. If it isn't infected, there is no danger.

Be sure to take note of any changes in your cat's toilet habits such as straining, constipation or diarrhea. They can be symptoms of a wide variety of illnesses. If they don't clear up immediately, check the relevant entries in the illness section of this book and, if nec-essary, consult your veterinarian.

NUTRITION

For good health and appearance, vitality and long life, your cat requires a diet that provides the proper amounts of protein, fat, vitamins, minerals and other nutrients. At each major stage of your pet's life its nutritional needs change to reflect the changing needs of its body. A kitten requires a diet suited to rapid growth, the development of strong teeth and bones and well-functioning internal organs and metabolism. An adult cat needs a diet that provides energy and good nutrition to fuel a healthy body at its peak. Even an older cat that has begun to slow down with advancing age will enjoy vigorous good health longer if its special dietary requirements are met.

Although commercial cat foods have gained enormous popularity, homemade cat foods are still a popular alternative. Cat food you prepare yourself is just as satisfactory as long as it meets the cat's full nutritional requirements. These needs are broader than the animal's designation as a carnivore (meat eater) might suggest. In its wild, undomesticated state, the cat does subsist solely on small animals and birds, but because it consumes all its prey, including the stomach and intestines, its diet also includes quantities of undigested greens and grains. The domesticated cat needs these in its diet too. If you are going to prepare the food yourself, you will have to make a point of providing them.

• Every meal ought to contain some high protein food such as cooked fish, meat or fowl combined with cooked vegetables.

• Raw egg yolks are also an excellent source of protein and can be included in the diet two or three times a week.

• Vegetables should be ground and thoroughly mixed into the meal so the cat can't remove or ignore them.

• Occasionally include high fat foods such as whole or dry milk, meat fat, cheese and cream. These foods are also an excellent source of additional protein.

• For a healthy, lustrous coat, add a teaspoon of unsaturated cooking or salad oil to the cat's meal two or three times a week.

For reasons of health or safety, certain foods should be avoided entirely and others given only occasionally or in small quantities:

• Large amounts of raw egg whites and organs such as liver, kidney and heart can upset the cat's vitamin balance and lead to serious physical problems.

• Raw meat may contain parasites and should be cooked thoroughly before being served to the cat. (Pork and pork products should be avoided altogether.)

• Starch must also be well cooked.

• Fish and chicken bones are dangerous because they may splinter into sharp pieces and stick in the cat's throat.

Rather than prepare the cat's food themselves, many owners find it more convenient to feed it commercial cat food. These foods are perfectly fine as long as they are produced by a reputable company that stays abreast of current nutritional information and research. Most supermarkets and grocery stores offer a great variety of such foods for sale:

• Maintenance foods that provide a fully balanced diet for the adult cat. They are available in many different flavors, and come both in cans, where the food is already moistened with water, and the more economical dry form to which water can be added. Dry foods have become increasingly popular because they are resistant to spoiling and can be left in the cat's dish. Male cats, however, should not be given an all dry diet because it may aggravate their tendency to have urinary problems, particularly crystals in the urinary tract.

• Special formula foods. Some are specifically designed for older cats that have begun to slow down. Others are for cats that have suffered heart disease, stress or some other illness that requires a special diet. Your veterinarian will tell you when any of these special formulas are appropriate.

• Specialty foods in small cans that are intended to supplement or add variety to the cat's staple diet. These serve as a flavorful change, but since they do not provide a fully balanced diet by themselves, they should not be used as a replacement for maintenance foods.

To give your cat a variety of tastes and textures, you might try out various combinations of flavors, moist and dry maintenance foods and specialty brands. Once you have found the combination that suits the cat's taste and meets its total nutritional requirements, you probably won't have to vary from it. If the cat begins rejecting the food at some later time, you can experiment briefly to discover a more acceptable combination of flavors and types.

Dog food contains substantially less protein and fat than a cat requires and should not be used as a substitute for cat food. A cat fed a steady diet of dog food will develop vitamin or mineral deficiencies that will ultimately harm its nervous system.

Adult cats can get along on a single daily feeding. Still, it is preferable to feed them twice a day. Cats fed only once always seem to be looking for something to eat.

To determine the proper portion for each meal, you will have to consider such factors as the cat's size, age, general level of activity and whether it lives indoors or out. Be aware that most of these things are subject to change and the changes have to be provided for. During the winter months, for example, the outdoor cat must be fed more generously since it burns up more calories to keep itself warm.

The main thing to remember is that it is essential to the cat's health not to gain weight after it reaches maturity. Overweight cats are invariably less active and often develop weight-related health problems as they grow older. It is a matter of record that they have a significantly shorter life-span than cats maintained at the proper weight.

Obesity caused by steady overfeeding usually develops slowly, so it is not always apparent. The cat may only put on a pound or two a year. Nevertheless, you can easily estimate your pet's proper weight by examining the fat covering over its ribs:

• If you can't feel the individual ribs, the cat is too fat.

• If the ribs stick out so your fingers can go between them, the animal is too thin.

• If you can feel the ribs but can't stick your fingers between them, the cat is at the right weight.

In addition to giving your cat the right food, you should also make sure it always has access to fresh water. Water plays a vital role in maintaining health and can help prevent certain serious illnesses, particularly as the cat grows older. Place the water in a bowl near your pet's food dish and change it daily. To correct a common error, milk may be nearly the perfect food but it is no substitute for water in the cat's diet.

You should also add balanced vitamin and mineral supplements to the cat's diet several times a week. Unless your veterinarian recommends it, do not give your pet individual vitamins or minerals such as calcium. They can disturb its metabolic balance and impair its health.

Take note of any significant increase or decrease in your cat's food and water intake, as well as such digestive irregularities as diarrhea, constipation and vomiting. If they persist, you should consult your veterinarian immediately, particularly if they are accompanied by other symptoms. (See the **SYMPTOM RECOGNITION INDEX** on page 65.) Although these conditions can be caused by dietary or environmental factors, they may also indicate the cat is infected with parasites or has some other illness.

TRAINING

HOUSEBREAKING

The cat is an instinctively clean animal, so training it to become housebroken is usually a very simple matter. Even in its undomesticated state, it will dig a hole in the ground for its wastes, then cover them up with soil. Many young kittens learn to use a litter tray while they are still nursing by observing and imitating their mother.

If your new cat is not already housebroken, you can begin training it as soon as you get it home:

• Restrict the animal to one room. Put its litter tray in there with it.

• Gently place the cat in the tray at those times of the day when it is most likely to relieve itself—early in the morning, after each meal, following exercise and play and before it goes to sleep at night.

• Whenever the cat performs its toilet functions in the pan, praise it and give it some small treat.

• If it makes a mistake and creates a mess, discipline it with a loud "No!" then put it in the pan. It is neither necessary nor desirable to hit it. Striking your pet with a rolled up newspaper or heavy hand will only frighten it and may cause it to strike back to protect itself. Your hand should just be used to administer affection and reward. You will only confuse the animal if you also use it as an instrument of punishment.

• To be effective, the reward or punishment must come immediately so the cat can understand that it is a direct result of something it did. After only a few minutes go by, it will no longer sense any connection between the mess it created and the fact you are displeased with it. It is useless and confusing to the animal to discipline it in the morning, for example, for an error it made during the night. The cat will know that something is wrong but cannot possibly comprehend what it is.

• While housebreaking is proceeding and the cat still soils the floor, the soiled spots should be immediately cleaned to prevent the cat from returning to them. You can remove the odor that guides your pet to these spots by washing them thoroughly with white vinegar and water, then covering them over with a generous amount of baking soda. After three or four hours, the dry powder can be removed with a vacuum cleaner or broom.

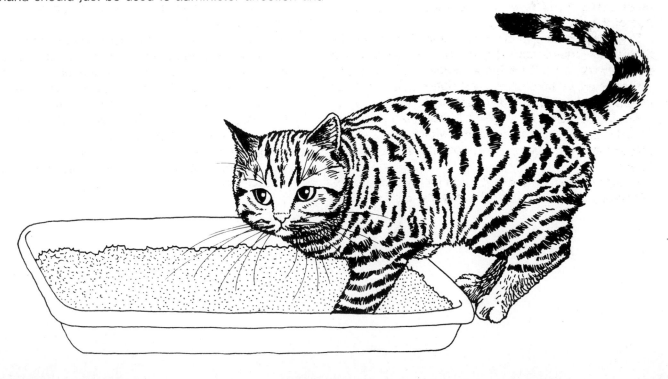

AGGRESSIVE BEHAVIOR

All cats are instinctively aggressive to some degree, particularly males. Watch young kittens at play, and notice how they roll around pawing and biting at one another, each trying to gain a clear advantage and force the others to surrender.

Such aggressiveness is both a natural and essential part of the animal's personality, one of the main reasons it survived as a species before it began to be domesticated. Without this trait it would not have been able to obtain food or defend itself from attack.

Domestication is the process by which the cat learns to live harmoniously with humans. By raising it from the time it is a kitten and giving it a secure home, good care, gentle handling and proper training, the owner can reduce the pet's natural aggressiveness to an acceptable level.

Taken as a whole, some breeds are more aggressive than others, but there is still a wide variation among cats of the same breed and even within members of the same litter. The variation is even greater in mixed breeds. For this reason, you should always evaluate an individual cat's aggressiveness before bringing it into your home. Page 19 tells you how to go about making this evaluation.

Some cats respond aggressively to the slightest provocation. Others remain even-tempered in almost any situation. But given significant provocation, any cat will become aggressive. Even owners who have had their pets for years and never seen the slightest expression of violence may one day find their cats reacting fiercely when placed in some particularly stressful set of circumstances.

To minimize this possibility, you should do your best to keep your cat from being provoked:

• Warn strangers that your pet may bite or scratch if it is bothered or feels threatened.

• If necessary, keep the cat away from people and animals you suspect may trigger a hostile response.

• Make sure it can always go someplace where nothing will bother it.

• Teach the children in your home that the cat is a living creature with feelings, not an inanimate toy. Youngsters who haven't learned this lesson will often tease or unintentionally hurt a family pet, forcing it to strike back to protect itself from some real or imagined threat. If necessary, keep your children from playing with the cat until they can comprehend that it must be treated with respect. If the children are too young to understand, you should probably postpone getting a cat until they are a bit more mature.

If you warn people about your pet's limits and minimize the situations that provoke it, aggressiveness probably will never become a serious problem.

GROOMING

To keep your pet healthy and looking its best, you will have to groom it regularly. It is best to begin while the cat is still young. Kittens are far more tolerant than adult cats of brushing and the like and adapt to it much more readily. Once a regular routine has been established, they will accept it willingly and come to relax and enjoy it. You will have to expend a bit more time and patience on a mature cat to bring it to this point, though eventually it too will come to accept grooming as an expected part of its daily routine.

BRUSHING

Since the cat's fur serves to protect it from the weather, its thickness normally varies with the seasons. The thickness of its coat is regulated by the temperature and the amount of sunlight to which it is exposed. Shedding is heaviest during the spring and summer months when there are the most hours of daylight. The fur is thickest during the winter months when the days are short. This explains why indoor cats living in artificial light tend to shed more or less uniformly throughout the year.

Regular brushing provides much better care for the cat's coat than the animal can give itself. Here are some points to keep in mind to do it properly:

• Brush your pet's fur for at least five or ten minutes every day. Long-haired cats should be brushed twice a day. This will untangle knots before they become matted and remove loose hairs that might otherwise be swallowed when the animal grooms itself with its tongue. Swallowed hairs can form into hair balls and cause digestive problems if not passed out of the cat's system. Older cats have an especially difficult time digesting swallowed hair, so they should be brushed with particular frequency. Regular brushing will also cut down on the number of unwelcome hairs you'll find scattered about your house and clothing.

• Brush the hair in the direction of growth. Go against the direction of growth before your final brushing to expose the underlayers to the brush and make the coat look attractively full and fluffy. Give as much attention to the stomach and inside of the legs as you do to the head, back and neck.

• Many long-haired cats grow hair between their toes, which frequently becomes matted with asphalt, vegetation and foreign objects. To save your pet discomfort, inspect the area each time you give it a brushing and clean the material away whenever necessary. If the problem becomes recurrent, keep the hair between the toes trimmed short.

• Long hair around the anus should also be kept short to prevent anal plugs.

• Every time you brush, make a point of looking closely at the skin beneath the fur. It should be clean and pliable with a healthy pinkish color. Bald spots, redness and blotches are never normal and indicate that something is wrong. They may be caused by any number of conditions including parasites, skin diseases, allergies, poor diet and reaction to stress. Watch such symptoms closely. If they persist or worsen, bring them to your veterinarian's attention.

• Also be on the lookout for foreign substances that have become tangled in your pet's hair. Cats are curious animals and often come home matted with paint, tar, chewing gum and the like. These substances can usually be dealt with best while they are still fresh and haven't yet become dried and crusted. Often they are water soluble and can easily be removed with soap and water.

• Areas matted with tar or other substances that are not soluble in water should be saturated with vegetable oil, then covered with bandages to keep the cat from licking at them. After about eight hours they ought to have softened enough to be removed with soap and water. It may be necessary to repeat the process if all the material doesn't wash away. When all of it finally has been removed, wash the entire area with soap and water, then rinse and dry it thoroughly.

• Never use cleaning fluid, turpentine or other strong solvents to clean matted fur. They will irritate the cat's skin and can poison the animal if absorbed into its body. If the fur is too badly matted to clean with soap and water or vegetable oil, have your veterinarian deal with it.

• It is never desirable and seldom necessary to remove matted hair by cutting it away. If it ever does become necessary, the matted area should be cut into small pieces in the direction of growth, not across it. This will take some time and patience, but these smaller pieces can then be combed or brushed from the coat without spoiling the cat's looks or depriving it of its natural protection. When large areas are affected, the cat should be brought to the vet.

• Occasionally, a cat's coat or feet may become soiled with toxic substances such as tar and paint. If they become absorbed into the animal's skin or enter the system through its mouth when it tries to clean itself, they may very well poison it. Should this happen, flush the poisons away as quickly as possible with large amounts of cool water. See **POISONING: CONTACT**, page 164, for the step-by-step procedure for dealing with this emergency.

• Never trim the cat's moustache or whiskers. The animal needs these delicate hairs to climb in and out of small spaces safely. If the hairs can pass through an opening without touching the sides, the cat knows its body will also be able to pass through.

BATHING

Cats are innately clean animals and do not require regular bathing. They certainly don't enjoy it. A healthy cat will not normally have a strong or offensive odor. If it does smell, it may have a disease or infection that should be treated by a veterinarian.

You should only have to bathe your cat if it has become excessively dirty as a result of its explorations or has encountered a skunk or some other source of strong smell. (Skunk smell is highly resistant to soap and water. The best way to remove it is by soaking the animal in tomato juice for several minutes, then bathing it as described below.) Kittens under six months old should not be bathed unless it is absolutely necessary. They are still susceptible to many illnesses and don't yet have much resistance to fight them off.

• Bathing should always be done indoors in a warm spot that is free of drafts.

• Try to get an assistant to hold the cat and keep it calm while you bathe it.

• Use a mild, non-detergent hand soap or a specially formulated cat soap available in pet shops.

• Wash the cat with a gentle stream of warm water. A hose or faucet is better than a spray, which may alarm the animal.

• Take special care to keep the soap out of the cat's eyes. If you don't have assistance, you may have to hold your pet down with one hand to prevent it from splashing soapy water into its eyes.

• After the fur has been cleaned, make sure to rinse away all traces of the soap to prevent irritation to the sensitive skin underneath.

• The cat should then be toweled down thoroughly and protected from drafts until it is completely dry. Keep it indoors while it is still wet. If you let it outside, it will probably want to roll around on the ground to dry itself. The hot summer sun can also cause heat exhaustion or sunstroke in a wet animal.

• When the cat is fully dry, give it a good brushing to remove all the loose hairs and restore the luster to its fur.

As an alternative to soap and warm water, the cat can be cleaned with a "dry bath." This is a commercial preparation available in pet shops that absorbs dirt and oil when applied to the skin, then is removed by brushing. It will do a reasonably good job of cleaning the cat and is preferable for kittens under six months old. If you decide to try this method, you might consider using ordinary cornstarch rather than the commercial preparation. It does the same job at a substantially lower cost.

EARS

Once a week the cat's ear flaps should be examined and, if necessary, cleaned. This is a relatively simple task, but there are a few important precautions to keep in mind: **Do not** use alcohol or other solvents on the cat's ears. **Do not** try to clean further inside the ear than you can actually see. The L-shape of the cat's ear canal offers natural protection to the delicate inner ear structures. For the same reason, **do not** pull on the ear flap while cleaning. This would straighten the ear canal and expose the inner ear structures to possible injury.

Before the cleaning begins, the cat must be restrained. It would be best to have an assistant hold down the cat for you, but if you are alone you should be able to do it yourself. The section on **RESTRAINTS,** page 177, details the procedures for both situations.

1. When the cat has been restrained, lift the ear flap and hold it firmly without pulling on it, while pressing the cat's head against your assistant.

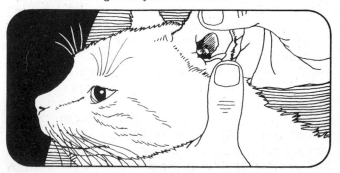

2. Carefully remove loose wax and debris from the ear and ear canal with dry cotton balls, then with cotton balls moistened in warm water.

3. Using a gentle, rotating motion, clean loose wax and debris from the ear folds and crevices with dry cotton-tipped swabs. Repeat with cotton-tipped swabs moistened in warm water. Repeat the process on the cat's other ear.

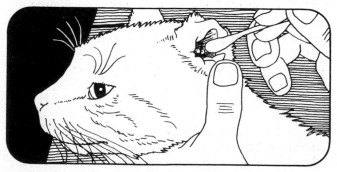

EYES

The cat's eyes should also be cleaned whenever necessary to prevent scabs or ulcerations from accumulated debris. Keep in mind that the cat has an opaque third eyelid that is not normally seen but which may come up to protect an injured eye. Should this happen, **do not** try to remove it or otherwise interfere with it.

Again, the cat must be restrained before the cleaning begins, either by an assistant or yourself. See the section on **RESTRAINTS,** page 177, for the right procedures.

1. Facing the cat, use a dry cotton ball to wipe away accumulated mucus and debris from the inside corner of the eye and the skin just below. Be gentle. **Do not** touch the eyeball.

2. Remove any remaining mucus or debris with a cotton ball moistened in warm water. The lower lid may be pulled down slightly to facilitate the cleaning. Repeat the process on the cat's other eye.

TEETH

The cat should also be inspected regularly for any signs of tooth decay or diseased gums. Cats predisposed to tooth problems often have trouble with their front teeth, especially the large incisors, and may not be able to bite and chew normally. If you smell a strong, unpleasant odor when you open its mouth, something is probably wrong and the cat should be taken to the veterinarian. Since abscesses, bleeding gums and lost teeth force the animal's body to fight constantly against infection, they have a seriously harmful effect and can eventually lead to anemia.

Make a particular point of checking that your pet's teeth are relatively free of tartar. If tartar is allowed to accumulate, the affected teeth may eventually be lost. Look for the characteristic green stains. If they are present, the cat should have its teeth cleaned by your vet. Some pets require a regular cleaning once a year to keep built-up tartar from becoming a problem.

NAILS

The sharp, curved claws on the cat's paws grow constantly but are usually worn down by the cat's normal activities. Pets that spend a lot of time outdoors walking and running over rough ground aren't commonly bothered by overly long nails. However, indoor cats and those that don't get very much exercise do require periodic nail-trimming. Claws that become too long break easily and are likely to become snagged on carpets, furniture and clothing. If the cat has to struggle to break free, it can cause painful damage to itself and may even lose the nail.

Cats that need it should have their claws clipped about once a month with professional clippers made for this purpose. You can ask your veterinarian to show you what to do or follow this relatively simple procedure:

Have someone help you restrain the cat on a plastic or metal tabletop. See **RESTRAINTS,** page 177.

1. Hold the paw in your hand, and taking each nail in turn, squeeze it at the base between your thumb and index finger. Leave just a slight excess of nail beyond your fingertips.

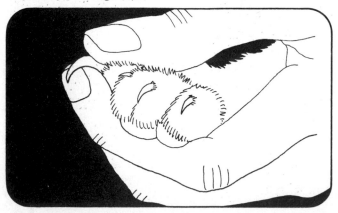

2. With your other hand, carefully clip the end of the nail, taking care not to clip the vein that enters the nail near the paw. If the cat's nails are translucent, a bright light will help you see this vein clearly. Should you have an accident, the bleeding can be stopped with direct pressure. See **BLEEDING: CUTS & WOUNDS,** page 121, for the proper procedure.

3. When you have finished the nails, trim the dew-claws. There may be more than one on each foot.

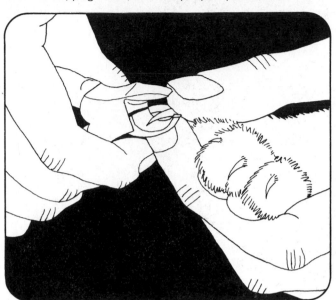

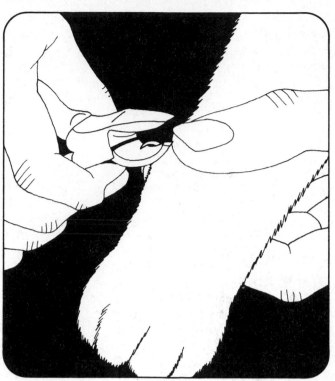

PARASITES

Fleas, ticks, lice and mites are among the common parasites that may infest your cat. Outdoor cats are especially susceptible to these pests, particularly if they spend a lot of time in contact with dogs and other cats. These parasites attach themselves to the cat's hair or skin, then feed on the animal and begin to reproduce themselves. Some of them reproduce so quickly that they can seriously infest your pet in a very short time. Parasites are not only annoying to the cat but potentially dangerous. They can cause anemia and spread disease to the animal and the other members of your family.

Look closely for evidence of parasites on the skin and fur whenever you groom your pet. Even if you can't find anything, you should suspect it is infested if it constantly scratches at its fur, shakes its head vigorously or rubs its body against corners and other hard surfaces.

Parasites can neither be prevented nor eliminated by bathing. If your cat is contaminated, you will have to treat it with the appropriate medication. Make sure the medicine is made specifically for use on cats and follow the accompanying directions carefully. Do not use home remedies—they may contain injurious chemicals.

When a cat has parasites, you can assume that its bedding is also infested. Discard the bedding or wash it thoroughly and make a point of keeping the fresh bedding particularly clean until the parasites are gone. You will also have to decontaminate all the areas your pet frequents. Only a small percentage of the fleas, lice and mites in the cat's environment are on its body at any one time. Typically, these parasites will jump on the cat as it passes by, feed for awhile, then jump back off.

For more detailed instruction on how to treat specific parasites, see **PARASITES: EXTERNAL,** page 97.

CARS

Most cat's don't have any difficulty traveling in cars once they become accustomed to being in a moving vehicle. If possible, start getting your cat used to it while it is still a kitten.

To begin, have the cat sit in your parked car for a few minutes at a time. Then gradually increase the time you leave it there. When your pet seems at ease, start running the engine while it sits there. Now begin taking it for short rides that gradually become longer. After a-while, it should be perfectly comfortable and enjoy its outings thoroughly.

There are a number of precautions to keep in mind that will ensure your pet's safety and comfort.

• Make sure the cat always wears its license and identification tag when you take it driving. Should you somehow become separated, the person who finds your cat will need that information to get it back to you.

• Never leave the cat in a closed or even partially closed automobile on a sunny day. Even if the temperature is only moderate, the inside of a closed car can quickly heat up to 100°F. (37.7°C.) or more.

• On longer trips, try to bring along the cat's regular bedding and food dishes. They will help it feel more secure about being away from home.

MOTION SICKNESS

Younger cats under about a year old are sometimes sensitive to motion and may start to salivate, drool, retch and vomit when taken out for a drive. These symptoms usually start slowly, but then progress more rapidly, continuing throughout the ride and for some time afterward. Some cats outgrow this condition after a while. Others do not.

If your cat is subject to motion sickness, your vet-erinarian can prescribe Dramamine or some other medication that may keep it from becoming ill. Tranquilizers can also help a cat that is made anxious or frightened by travel. To be effective, the medication will have to be administered several hours before the trip. Withholding food and water doesn't usually keep a sensitive cat from feeling dizzy and nauseous, but it will reduce the mess if the animal does become ill.

PLANES, TRAINS AND BUSES

All forms of public transportation that will accept cats require that they be placed in a cat carrier or other suitable enclosure. This rule is necessary to prevent the cat from becoming a nuisance and to protect the other passengers from being harmed by an animal that turns suddenly vicious out of fright. It is also necessary to protect the cat itself from being hurt if the vehicle has to make an abrupt stop.

Travel carriers come in all different sizes from small boxes to large crates and cages. Make sure the one you choose is large enough to allow your cat to stand on all four legs and turn around comfortably.

• It should be sturdily constructed of easy to clean materials such as plastic, metal or wood.

• To keep it from opening in transit, it should be equipped with a sturdy hinged top or door that is held closed with several fasteners and a belt. It should also have a rounded top and a strong carrying handle.

• Check that the enclosure is well-ventilated with small openings around the sides toward the bottom. Larger openings must be protected with screens or bars. The cat may harm itself if it is able to poke its paw through. Since cats seem to feel more secure in potentially frightening situations if they cannot see or be seen, larger openings should be fitted with curtains to limit the animal's view of the outside and protect it from curious bystanders.

• Write your name and address clearly on the outside of the carrier in case you become separated from your pet.

• If the cat will be riding in the baggage compartment, also write any special handling or feeding instructions on the outside of the box, along with the words "LIVE ANIMAL" printed in large letters.

• When you take your pet on an extended trip that requires it to spend considerable time in the enclosure,

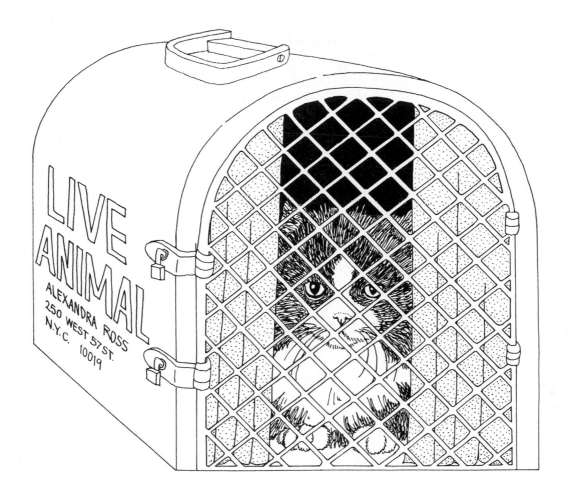

line the bottom fully with shredded paper. The paper will give the cat a soft surface to lie on and also absorb its urine. To cut down on the amount of waste, don't give the cat food or water for several hours before the trip begins. Unless the weather is particularly hot or the ride lasts longer than 12 hours, withhold water until you reach your destination. On longer trips, limit the cat to small amounts of food and drink.

If you are going abroad and plan to take your cat with you, find out whether the country you will be visiting has any travel restrictions about pets. Regulations vary widely from one country to another. Some only require a health certificate stating that the cat has been recently inoculated against rabies and other infectious diseases. Others insist that it be quarantined for as long as six months.

LEAVING THE CAT BEHIND

If it isn't feasible to take the cat along with you on your travels, make early plans to leave it at a reliable cattery. Your veterinarian ought to be able to recommend one or may be able to board your pet in his own facility.

• The cattery you select should be operated by professionals who will provide clean and comfortable housing for your pet, feed and care for it properly, give it plenty of exercise and return it to you in good health. Don't make final arrangements until you visit the place and check its facilities yourself. If the cats you see there don't look healthy and happy, find someplace else.

• Before leaving your pet at the cattery, make sure

it has been immunized against infectious diseases within the past year. It will be in unusually close contact with many other animals while you are away and might be exposed to infection.

• Alert your veterinarian that you are leaving your cat at the cattery. Tell him that if an emergency arises he has your permission to treat the pet. Write down the vet's name, address and telephone numbers and give them to the cattery operator. Also give him a note detailing any special requirements about diet, medication and the like.

THE FACTS OF LIFE

SEXUAL MATURITY

The female cat usually reaches sexual maturity when she is between five and seven months old. From that time on she will usually come into season twice each year, typically in the spring and fall.

There may be two or more heat cycles during a season, each lasting about two to three weeks. Certain temporary changes in the cat will tell you when it has started:

• Her voice becomes loud and demanding, sounding almost as though she were in pain. Her instinctive purpose here, of course, is to attract the male.

• She may either grow particularly affectionate, rolling over at your feet, or become nervous and edgy, even to the point of biting at your hands and feet.

• Her vulva swells and you may find her licking at it constantly.

If the cat is bred, the cycle will end within four days. If she is not bred, the symptoms may recur several times until she is no longer in heat. Also keep in mind that while she remains in heat she is more likely to try to run out of the house, and since males may be attracted to her scent, she may be accidentally bred if you let her outside.

Each heat cycle has several distinct phases:

• The first phase lasts about two to six days. During this time the female is affectionate but not yet receptive to the male.

• The second phase lasts nine to ten days, during which you may find her presenting her rear end and treading in place with her back paws. The cat is fertile and receptive, and if she is bred she will most likely conceive. A cat may breed numerous times during this period and may conceive more than once. The litter of kittens may have different fathers.

• During the third phase, which lasts two to six days, she becomes increasingly less receptive and less likely to conceive if she is bred.

• Between cycles, these symptoms may disappear for a while, then reappear again a few days later.

The male cat reaches sexual maturity at about 11 months, when he is almost fully grown. The signs are usually quite clear:

• He becomes highly territorial, marking out his area by spraying objects with his urine. The purpose here is to attract females and warn other males away. If another male dares to intrude upon his domain, he is quite likely to fight with him. The strong, offensive odor of this urine is difficult to remove. Should your male spray your furniture or painted walls, they may be ruined.

• He shows a greater tendency to roam and becomes much more aggressive with cats encountered along the way, particularly other males.

THE CAT POPULATION EXPLOSION

Literally millions of unwanted kittens are born each year. A large number come from unaltered strays, but they are not the root of the problem. The majority are produced by household pets whose owners have allowed them to breed not because they wanted kittens but because they erroneously thought this was the "right" thing to do.

There is no evidence to suggest it is either more "natural" or desirable for a female cat to have at least one litter before she is altered. This view attributes highly questionable human-like feelings and emotions to the animal. From everything that is known, a cat's sexual behavior is strictly in response to instinct. Nor is there any basis for concluding that neutering a cat has a negative effect on its health or well-being. What

is certain is that this one litter, multiplied by millions of cats, produces a problem of enormous proportions.

Many owners also permit their females to breed because of the marvelous opportunity it gives their children to witness the miracle of birth. While there is no doubt that this can be an extremely worthwhile experience, it should not be provided at the expense of the kittens.

Before allowing your pet to mate, you should be prepared to find a good home for its kittens if you don't want to keep them yourself. This is often more difficult than you might expect.

Friends and neighbors who indicate they may be willing to take the kittens off your hands often change their minds by the time they are born, so you will need more than a few casual "maybes" to find them good homes. And you had better start looking early, as soon as you know the mother is pregnant. Ask your friends to ask their friends. Advertise in your local newspaper. Post notices on the public bulletin boards in your neighborhood. Have your youngsters tell their schoolmates. Keep in mind that the kittens will not be ready to leave their mother until they are six or eight weeks old and until then you will have to take care of them yourself.

If you are lucky, you may find responsbile, loving homes for all your unwanted kittens. If you aren't— and the enormous overpopulation of cats makes this likely—then you may have a troublesome problem on your hands.

The Society for the Prevention of Cruelty to Animals (SPCA), Humane Society and other organizations devoted to the well-being of pets can offer only limited help. They simply don't have the facilities to house the enormous number of unwanted, lost and abandoned cats and dogs left at their doorstep. And despite their effective organizational and promotional resources, they succeed in placing only a small percentage of the animals they are able to shelter. For lack of a more satisfactory alternative, they are usually forced to put the remainder to a painless death. To illustrate the magnitude of the problem, of the 130,000 animals passing through one large animal shelter in a major city, only 15,000 were adopted or recovered by their owners. The remaining 115,000 had to be destroyed.

Many pet owners set their unwanted animals free, preferring to give them a chance at survival rather than subjecting them to euthanasia. This may seem to be a humane solution to the problem. It isn't. The facts are that few cats thrust out on their own are able to feed and care for themselves and almost none live out their normal life expectancy. Those that aren't soon killed by automobiles gradually deteriorate and ultimately succumb to the effects of malnutrition, injury and illness.

Veterinarians and other animal health care specialists who see and treat these abandoned pets agree that releasing a cat to make its own way in the city, suburbs or country is both cruel and inhumane. Even though these specialists are personally repulsed by the idea of euthanasia, many of them will tell you that it is, sadly, the lesser of two repugnant evils.

There is, of course, a better way. Don't let your pet breed if you don't want the kittens or won't be able to take care of them. A number of alternative methods are available.

If you think your female cat may have been bred because you found her with a male during her fertile period, you can consult your veterinarian immediately. If it is still early enough, the vet may be able to prevent or terminate the pregnancy. Unfortunately, this alternative isn't always effective. An owner may not realize the cat is pregnant until it is too late for anything to be done about it.

Conception can also be prevented by prescription medication that will temporarily postpone or end the heat cycle. This method is commonly used on pets whose fertile periods come into conflict with their owners' plans to enter them in cat shows. It is not intended as a lifelong form of birth control.

Almost all pet specialists agree that there is only one truly effective solution to the tragic overpopulation of unwanted kittens. Owners must be understanding and responsible enough to neuter any male or female cats they do not want bred.

NEUTERING YOUR CAT

The veterinarian can neuter your cat at any age, but the best time would be before it reaches sexual maturity. Females should have the operation when they are around five and a half or six months old. Males ought to be slightly older.

The surgery is painless and relatively simple and safe. It involves castrating the male and removing the uterus and ovaries from the female. The cat will only have to stay in the hospital a day or two, then recover quietly at home for about a week.

Consult your veterinarian about his fee. Because the operation is somewhat more involved and time-consuming for a female, it usually costs somewhat more. But veterinarians have traditionally kept the expense down to as little as possible to encourage pet owners to have the procedure done. Some communities also have programs that make this surgery available to eligible pet owners at reduced cost. Your local SPCA or Humane Society should be able to tell you if such a program exists in your area.

Neutering the female ends her heat cycle but has no negative effect on the cat's personality. She should become an even nicer and more tranquil pet and no longer desire to run off every six months. As additional benefits, she is also likely to live longer and develop fewer of the health problems common to unaltered females during middle and later life.

A male that is altered before it reaches sexual maturity will become more even-tempered and affectionate and less likely to roam, spray its urine and get into fights with other cats. If the surgery is postponed until later, he may still show the urge to roam, fight and mark his territory with urine, although the urine will no longer have such an offensive odor. He may at first continue to show his usual sexual habits because of the hormones that temporarily remain in his system, but this will end within a month.

Some cats, especially males, tend to gain weight after neutering. This can be controlled by providing sufficient exercise and adjusting the diet as necessary.

BREEDING YOUR CAT

If you decide you do want your female to have kittens, the time to breed her is during the second phase of her heat cycle.

Some time before then, have her examined by your veterinarian, so he can determine if she is in good health and begin any special care she may require.

• Bring along a specimen of the cat's stool in a closed container. The vet will want to analyze it for evidence of internal parasites. If your pet is infected, she should be treated immediately. Many parasites can be passed to kittens while they are still inside the mother, and it is very difficult to do anything for infected newborn kittens because they don't have the strength to withstand the necessary medication.

• Treatment for fleas and other external parasites should also be started before breeding. They can produce potentially fatal anemia in young kittens that are heavily infested.

• You should also have your female reimmunized against infectious diseases, even if she has already had her regular series of vaccinations. The greater the mother's immunity, the greater the immunity of her kittens when they are born and during the crucial first weeks when they are still nursing.

The period of pregnancy lasts about 63 days. During most of this time the mother can be treated quite normally. You should, however, make a particular point of giving her adequate exercise and a properly balanced diet. They are essential both to her own health and the health of her kittens.

For the first month of pregnancy, maintain the mother on her normal portions of food. After that, put out extra food between regular meals so she won't become hungry. If you prefer, you can gradually increase the portions at each regular feeding so that she is getting about twenty-five percent more by the time the kittens are due. Also be sure to give her abundant amounts of fresh water throughout her pregnancy.

From 45 days after conception until their birth, the kittens are growing rapidly within the mother, drawing all their food from her as well as the vitamins, calcium and other minerals they need to develop properly. The mother can only supply them with what she receives in her diet along with whatever reserves she may have stored up in her body. If her food or calcium supply is inadequate, the kittens will begin to draw on this reserve and she will gradually lose weight and begin to look poorly during the last stages of pregnancy and right after the kittens are born.

For this reason, it is important to supplement the pregnant and nursing mother's diet with fresh milk and the vitamins and minerals prescribed by your veterinarian. If her calcium is not replaced as quickly as it is being used to form the kittens' bones and provide them with milk for nursing, the mother may develop eclampsia (milk fever), a serious disorder that can be fatal.

The symptoms of eclampsia are panting, anxiety, muscular tremors and twitches (particularly on top of the head) and an extreme fever that may reach as high as 109°F. (42.7°C.). If left untreated, they may quickly progress to convulsions and coma.

Should your female contract eclampsia and develop the characteristic high fever, you will have to reduce her body temperature at once to 103°F. (39.4°C.). Immerse or hose her in cold water, then wrap her in cold, wet sheets and pack her head in ice. As soon as the fever subsides, call your veterinarian for further treatment. Once the crisis has been passed, the mother will have to be removed from the litter and the kittens raised as orphans. Eclampsia tends to recur, so affected females should not be allowed to breed again.

During the last week or ten days of pregnancy, discourage your cat from running, jumping from high places and other strenuous exercise. Abortion can occur any time after the cat conceives as a result of hormonal, nutritional or hereditary problems as well as from trauma and infection of the uterus, but it is especially likely to happen in the later stages.

Should your cat abort, fetal material will be expelled from the birth canal and you are likely to find blood and stringy mucus on her vulva or the ground. Always consult your veterinarian immediately if you suspect your cat has aborted. An incomplete abortion can lead to serious health problems.

QUEENING (DELIVERY)

A week or two before the kittens are due, prepare a queening box for the mother to give birth in.

• It should be about twice as large as the cat's usual bed, so she will have enough room to lie down by herself on one side while the litter remains on the other.

• Make sure the sides are high enough to keep the kittens from falling or climbing out.

• Line the bottom with torn newspapers, and replace them as they become dirtied.

• Place the box somewhere in the house away from heavy traffic where it can still be closely watched. Select a spot that is relatively dark or that can be darkened. Cats prefer to be secluded from the light when they have their young.

• Have the expectant mother spend some time in the box so she can become used to it. If she doesn't come to feel at home there, she will probably have the litter where she usually sleeps.

• Should this happen, do not move her to the box until she has completed delivery and all the kittens

have been born. Interruptions should always be kept to a minimum. They can stop, inhibit or change the instinctive birth process.

Queening commonly takes place at night and often begins with a period of anxiety and restlessness.

• The cat will seem unusually listless, fidgety and uncomfortable, then she will probably begin to dig in the box or try to hide in a closet or dark corner. This phase normally lasts from several hours to 24 hours.

• When active contractions begin, they will be evident by the way the cat strains and tenses her stomach muscles.

• After a quarter hour or so, she may deliver a fluid-filled sac, then stop her efforts and begin to walk around as if everything were normal. Eventually, she will return to active labor.

• The first kitten may be born in as little as 15 minutes or as long as an hour. Let the mother proceed at her own pace. Do not distract or interrupt her. Watch only from a distance.

• The kitten may come out either head first or tail first. Both ways are perfectly normal.

• It may be born bullet-shaped and enclosed in a sac of membranes filled with fluid. The mother's instinctive response is to chew the membranes open and lick the kitten to stimulate breathing. Once the kitten begins to move, the mother will probably chew the umbilical cord and eat the membranes.

• If the kitten is born free of membranes, they will come along right behind it with the umbilical cord. The mother will also eat the membranes after she licks the kitten.

• Between births, you may see a green discharge, possibly tinged with red or black blood. This is a natural part of the birth process and nothing to become alarmed about.

• The time between kittens can range from 30 minutes to two hours. Once the time pattern is established, the mother usually stays to it. While she is still actively involved in giving birth, she probably won't pay too much attention to the kittens that have already been

born. If she does not resume active contractions following the normal period between births, it is usually safe to assume all the kittens have been delivered.

Queening presents almost no danger to the mother, but certain complications may imperil the kittens if not dealt with properly.

Consult your veterinarian if contractions continue for several hours without a kitten being born or if they stop after one or two kittens are delivered and more still appear to be inside the mother.

Occasionally, a kitten may emerge only partially from the birth canal and the mother is unable to complete the delivery. Should this happen, restrain the mother (see **RESTRAINTS,** page 177), then grasp the kitten with a dry towel and pull it gently in a downward direction toward the mother's feet. As she strains during contractions, pull somewhat harder. As she relaxes between contractions, simply maintain your hold on the kitten so it is not pulled back in. The kitten can usually be delivered like this without harming the mother, although there is a good chance that it will be born dead.

Should the mother fail to free a kitten from the closed sac of membranes you will have to do it yourself within five minutes to keep the kitten alive. Use dry paper towels to pull the sac open, then rub the kitten gently to stimulate breathing.

Watch the mother closely for two weeks after queening and report any symptoms of serious illness to the veterinarian. Some vaginal bleeding is normal for one or two days after giving birth. Call your vet if the bleeding seems heavy or persists for more than a few days. The membranes she has eaten may take away her appetite for a day or so or cause a brief bout of vomiting or diarrhea. There is no cause for concern unless these symptoms continue.

The first milk newborn kittens take from their mother is rich in colostrum, a substance that temporarily passes on to them her immunity to disease. It is very important that each kitten in the litter gets a share of this first milk. Watch the kittens as they nurse to make sure all have their turn. If any one of them doesn't, remove the other kittens from the queening box and put that one to the mother's breast.

It is also important to the mother's health that her mammary glands be adequately drained. They may not be if the kittens aren't taking enough milk, or if they become injured or infected or don't dry up naturally. (The breasts are a particularly fertile area for infection during and after pregnancy.) During the period when the mother is nursing her litter, feel her breasts every day to make sure they are still soft and pliable.

If they are hard and caked and you can feel a solid mass inside them, consult your veterinarian. He may tell you to apply warm compresses for 15 minutes three or four times a day.

Should the mother develop mastitis (an infection of the mammary glands), the breasts will be hot, red and painful when touched, and the mother may resist her kittens' efforts to nurse. In more advanced cases, the cat may develop a fever, lose her appetite and show other symptoms of systemic infection. The glands may also form pus pockets and abscess to the outside of the breast. Call your veterinarian immediately at the first sign of any of these symptoms. The kittens will probably have to be taken away from the mother and raised as orphans.

In a normal situation where nothing goes wrong, the mother will continue to nurse her kittens for three or four weeks after they are born. Her need for food now will be even greater than it was during pregnancy. You may find it necessary to give her more than twice her usual portions. Make sure that extra food is always available to her during this period so she need never go hungry.

TAKING CARE OF AN ABANDONED KITTEN

Occasionally, a new mother will move one of her kittens away from the other members of the litter and make a great point of keeping it there. This usually means she believes something is wrong with it. She is usually right. Unless the kitten is cared for separately, it will almost certainly die. You should make some attempts to place the kitten back in the litter, but don't be surprised if your efforts fail. If it is to survive, you will have to raise it yourself as an orphan. On those rare occasions when the mother shows no interest in caring for any of her kittens, you will have to do the same thing with the entire litter.

The abandoned kitten should be placed in its own box in a draft-free room where the temperature can be maintained at a constant 85°F. to 90°F. (29.4°C. to 32.2°C.). If it is not kept at this temperature and becomes cold or chilled, it will inevitably die. Chilling is one of the most common causes of death in newborn kittens because they are unable to regulate their own body temperature.

Feed the kitten with a formula consisting of one egg yolk mixed in eight ounces of milk or a commercially prepared formula specifically made for orphaned kittens. Warm the food and feed it to the kitten with an eyedropper or dosing syringe. Give it as much as it will take five or six times a day. When it has had enough, its stomach will feel comfortably full but not distended or swollen. If it isn't getting enough to eat, it will whine and move restlessly about its box.

An abandoned kitten will also have to be stimulated to perform its normal toilet functions. This is best accomplished by rubbing a cotton swab dipped in mineral oil around its anus three or four times a day or inserting it about half an inch. After about four weeks the kitten should be able to take care of itself and the stimulation will no longer be necessary.

WEANING AND FEEDING KITTENS

For the first three or four weeks of life, kittens are nourished exclusively by their mother's milk. After a month or so, the process of weaning can be begun by giving them a little milk in a saucer. If it's necessary, you can encourage them to drink by gently pushing their faces toward the saucer. If that doesn't work, dip your finger in the milk, then place it in their mouths so they can suck on it. It won't take them long to learn to suck with their faces down rather than up, and once they get the idea of sucking from the saucer, they will soon begin to lap.

Over the course of the next week or so, the milk can be gradually thickened with pablum or cereal grains to make it more solid. As the kittens adjust to their new food, it can be thickened still more with ground meat and egg yolks or a commercial kitten food. Kittens sometimes show an interest in what their mother is being given to eat. As long as this food is soft and moist, it is perfectly safe for them.

As the kittens take progressively less nourishment from the mother, her food portions should be gradually cut back to what they were before she became pregnant. Reducing the amount of the mother's food also reduces the amount of milk she produces. This will help wean the kittens by forcing them to find their food elsewhere.

By the time they are six to eight weeks old, the kittens should be fully weaned and on a solid diet. To ensure their proper growth, make certain their food is especially high in protein and rich in the necessary vitamins and minerals. Until they are about ten weeks old, feed them three or four times a day. After that, two or three meals a day will suffice.

THE BREEDS OF CATS

This section provides basic information on the appearance, temperament and special needs of the most popular breeds of cats in this country. It is intended to give the prospective buyer some general insight into each type of cat as it exists outside the show ring in its more characteristic role as family pet. This emphasis is more in keeping with the purpose of this book than the highly detailed "standards" formulated by experts to describe characteristics found in some hypothetically perfect specimen of a breed.

When you read these descriptions, keep in mind that the members of the same breed are far from identical. There are often substantial variations in size, color, hair length and texture and all the other physical characteristics. Although these variations can be crucially significant when it comes to championship breeding and show competition, they don't necessarily have any real bearing on whether or not a particular cat is suitable as a family pet.

Also keep in mind that there are wide variations in temperament among cats belonging to the same breed. The personality of an individual cat is shaped by many things, including such circumstantial factors as the kind of home it came from, the kind it goes to and the early handling and training it has received. Very few valid generalizations can be made about temperament except in the broadest statistical sense. In fact, the variability **within** breeds may be even greater than that **between** breeds. Prospective buyers must always evaluate each cat's personality individually. After you have decided what breed you want and are looking at a particular cat, turn to page 19 and follow the procedure given there for assessing that animal's temperament.

ABYSSINIAN

APPEARANCE

An elegant, medium-sized shorthair with a distinctive silky, dense rabbit-like coat. It has a long heart-shaped head with large, pointed ears. The graceful body is slender and sleek, with small feet and a long, tapering tail. The Abyssinian's large, almond-shaped eyes are gold or green.

COLOR

Ruddy brown or red. The Abyssinian's coat is unique in that each hair is ticked with two or three bands of black or dark brown. Kittens are often born with dark coats that change to the characteristic colors as the animal matures.

CHARACTERISTICS

A very old breed believed to be the sacred cat of ancient Egypt. It was first brought to the West from Abyssinia a little more than a hundred years ago. Introduced into the United States in the 1930s, it has become the third most popular breed in North America, exceeded only by the Siamese and Burmese. Gentle, sometimes to the point of timidity, it makes an affectionate, playful pet, particularly devoted to its owner. It is an unusually intelligent animal and can be taught to fetch balls and do other dog-like tricks. Its short, close coat makes it easy to care for. The Abyssinian is an active cat and dislikes being confined too closely.

AMERICAN SHORTHAIR (DOMESTIC SHORTHAIR)

APPEARANCE

A powerfully built, muscular cat of medium to large size. It has a large head with a short, broad face and round, wide-set eyes. The fairly long ears are also set widely apart and are somewhat rounded at the tips. The tail and heavily muscled legs are both moderately long. The coat is short, thick and hard.

COLOR

Black, white, cream, blue or red—either in solid colors or in any combination of any patterns. White may be tipped with black, red or blue. Tabby pattern, calico and tortoiseshell are also found.

CHARACTERISTICS

A very old American breed that, according to one story, may have come to the United States with the first pilgrims. Always popular, it has been a permanent resident of American farms and homes for hundreds of years, where it has served as a dependable mouser and loyal, affectionate family pet. It is a particularly hardy, strong, healthy cat with an even temper and high intelligence.

AMERICAN WIREHAIR

APPEARANCE

A medium to large cat with curly whiskers and ear hairs and a unique hard, wiry, tightly curled coat. Its round head has prominent cheeks, a well-developed muzzle and medium-sized widely spaced ears that are slightly rounded at the ends. The large round eyes are usually brilliant gold but may be green, blue-green, hazel or deep blue. The strong body rests on muscular legs and has a rounded rump and a tail that tapers to a rounded tip.

COLOR
White, black, light blue, deep red or cream—either in solid colors or combinations. White may be tipped with black, blue or red. Also occurs in tabby patterns.

CHARACTERISTICS
A relatively new breed produced by mutation, the American Wirehair is an active, agile, especially curious cat.

BALINESE

APPEARANCE
A long-haired version of the Siamese, this handsome, medium-sized cat has a fine-textured, medium-long coat with the distinctive Siamese coloration and pattern. Its long, wedge-shaped head has broad, pointed ears and vivid blue almond-shaped eyes that slant toward the nose. The long, graceful, elegant body is fine-boned but firmly muscled. The long plumed tail tapers to a point.

COLOR
Cream or fawn, gradually darkening on the back. The face, ears, legs, feet and tail are marked with well-defined seal, blue, chocolate, lilac or red points. Kittens are born white and darken as they mature.

CHARACTERISTICS
A very recent breed developed in the 1950s from long-haired mutant Siamese. The cat was named Balinese not because it originated in Bali, but to establish its distinctiveness as a separate breed. It is a gentle, affectionate, particularly curious and intelligent animal, generally less demanding than its Siamese forebears and with a somewhat softer voice. Loyal and devoted to its owner, it makes a companionable, playful pet that can be taught simple tricks like a dog. Though its coat is fairly long, it is considerably shorter than a Persian's, so needs less grooming.

BIRMAN

APPEARANCE
A most impressive-looking cat, with a long, silky coat, full mane and long, bushy tail. Its long, rather thick body rests on medium, sturdy legs. The strong head is wide and rounded, with full cheeks, medium-long ears and almost round blue eyes.

COLOR
Cream, gradually darkening on the back. The face, ears, legs, feet and tail are pointed with seal, blue, chocolate or lilac. The paws are marked with distinctive white "gloves."

CHARACTERISTICS
Known as the sacred cat of Burma, the Birman served as a temple guardian and was believed to be the reincarnation of Burmese priests. It was first brought to Europe in the 1920s. Almost all the European examples of the breed perished during World War II. Only recently introduced into the United States, its good looks and gentle, affectionate nature are making it increasingly popular here. The Birman is a friendly, intelligent cat with a small, pleasant voice and a particularly good temperament. Its fur does not mat but does require daily grooming.

BOMBAY

APPEARANCE
A muscular medium-sized cat with a distinctive short, satiny coat that shines with an almost patent leather sheen. Its rounded head has a full face, short muzzle and wide-set, medium-size ears that are somewhat rounded at the tips. The round, widely spaced eyes range in color from yellow to deep copper. The tail is straight and moderately long.

COLOR
Jet black with no markings.

CHARACTERISTICS
A hybrid developed by crossing the Burmese with the black American Shorthair.

BRITISH SHORTHAIR

APPEARANCE
A medium to large cat with a powerful, muscular body and short, dense coat. It has a short, strong neck with prominent cheeks and a short muzzle. The medium-sized ears are widely spaced with slightly rounded tips. Depending on coat color, the large, round eyes may be copper, green, yellow, hazel or sapphire blue.

COLOR

Solid shades of black, blue, red, cream or white. Also found with tabby patterned, tortoiseshell and spotted coats.

CHARACTERISTICS

Developed by crossing native British cats with Persians. A placid animal, it is very easy to handle and serves as a good family pet.

BURMESE

APPEARANCE

A sturdy, compact medium-sized cat with a velvety short coat, well-muscled body and short, rounded, wedge-shaped head. The large ears are widely separated and slightly rounded at the tips. The tail is medium-long and rounded at the end. Its almond-shaped eyes range from yellow to gold.

COLOR

Seal brown, gradually lightening toward the belly. May also be blue, red, cream, lilac, champagne or tortoiseshell. Kittens are born with lighter coats that gradually darken within the first year.

CHARACTERISTICS

This lively, alert cat originated not in Burma but the United States, where it was developed from Siamese hybrids in the 1930s. It is an affectionate, gentle, sociable pet that is much less demanding than its Siamese ancestors. Kittens are especially active.

COLORPOINT SHORTHAIR

APPEARANCE

Each hair on the fine-textured, glossy coat of this strikingly beautiful cat is tipped with clearly defined points of another color. In all other respects it is virtually identical to the Siamese. It has a long, wedge-shaped head with large, broad, pointed ears and vivid blue slanted eyes. The long, slender body is both graceful and muscular, with slim legs and a long, tapered tail.

COLOR

White tipped with deep red, gray or apricot. Cream with brown points. Blue-white tipped with blue-gray. The tips may form ghost stripes and may occasionally be mottled with one or more contrasting colors.

CHARACTERISTICS

A hybrid resulting from a cross between the Siamese and American Shorthair, this affectionate, sociable, highly intelligent cat makes a fine house pet. Like the Siamese, it is a particularly talkative animal, with a loud, unusual voice that some people find rather unpleasant.

EGYPTIAN MAU

APPEARANCE

A powerfully built cat of medium size, with a long, lithe body and slim, graceful legs. The wedge-shaped head has light green or amber almond-shaped eyes and large, widely set, moderately pointed ears that are somewhat tufted. The long tail tapers toward the end. The hind legs are longer than the front. Its moderately long coat is fine, silky and lustrous.

COLOR

The Silver Mau has silver fur marked with distinctive black spots and bands. The Bronze Mau has tawny fur marked with bronze spots and bands. Also seen in silver, brown and smoke.

CHARACTERISTICS

Though its ancestry may go back as far as ancient Egypt, this elegant breed was first developed in the United States from Egyptian cats brought here from Cairo in the 1950s. (A slightly different version was independently developed in Britain even more recently.) Much like a Siamese, only with a softer voice. Somewhat difficult to handle and not well-suited to homes with young children.

EXOTIC SHORTHAIR

APPEARANCE

A strong, beautiful, dignified cat that is identical to the Persian in everything but its coat, which is dense, soft and considerably shorter. Its massive head is broad and rounded, with full cheeks, large round eyes and small wide-set ears that are rounded at the tips. The low-set body has large, round legs and a short, straight tail.

COLOR

Solid blue, red, cream or white. White may be tipped with black, red or blue. Also occurs in tabby patterns, calico and tortoiseshell.

CHARACTERISTICS

A hybrid produced by crossing the Persian with the

American Shorthair, the Exotic Shorthair is the perfect choice for anyone who enjoys the fine characteristics of the Persian but does not have the time or inclination to provide the considerable grooming it requires. Like the Persian, it is an affectionate, gentle, even-tempered animal but does not particularly enjoy being handled.

HAVANA BROWN

APPEARANCE

A glossy shorthair with a long, graceful, muscular body. It has a long, narrow head with bright green oval eyes. The large ears are pointed, tilted forward and widely separated on the head. The Havana has brown whiskers and distinctive pink pads on its feet.

COLOR

A uniform rich, warm brown.

CHARACTERISTICS

Named for its brown, cigar-like color, this unusually intelligent and sweet-natured cat originated not in Cuba but in England, where it was developed from Siamese, Russian Blues and various other breeds. It was first recognized as a distinct breed only about twenty years ago, but has become increasingly popular since then. Responsive, affectionate and soft-voiced, it makes an excellent house pet. It is a particularly hardy and healthy animal.

HIMALAYAN

APPEARANCE

A strikingly beautiful cat that combines the thick, silky coat and full mane of the Persian with the colorings and markings of the Siamese. The broad, rounded head has large, expressive deep-blue eyes and small tufted ears that are set widely apart. The broad-chested body is set low on short, thick legs and has a full, thick tail.

COLOR

Cream with seal-colored points on the face, ears, legs, feet and tail. Bluish-white with blue points. Ivory with chocolate points. Glacial white with lilac points. Off-white with red points. Cream with tortoiseshell or blue-cream points. Kittens are uniformly pale at birth, but their colors deepen and the points emerge as they mature.

CHARACTERISTICS

Developed in the United States and Britain principally by crossing the Siamese with the Persian, the Himalayan has gained extraordinary popularity since it first gained recognition as a distinct breed in the 1950s. It is an affectionate, gentle, friendly cat, almost dog-like in its devotion to its family, although it may resent being handled by children. It does demand a fair amount of attention and, like all long-hairs, requires frequent grooming.

JAPANESE BOBTAIL

APPEARANCE

A lean, muscular medium-sized shorthair with a distinctive short, rigid "pom-pom" tail that is usually carried erect. The legs are long and slender, with the rear legs somewhat longer than the front. The long triangular head has high cheekbones, large, widely spaced ears and widespread oval eyes that slant toward the ears.

COLOR

Characteristically tricolor, consisting of white with distinct patches of black and red-orange. May also be black, red, white, black and white, red and white, tortoiseshell with black, red and cream.

CHARACTERISTICS

Known for hundreds of years in Japan, where it was thought to impart good fortune to its household, the Japanese Bobtail was first brought to the United States in 1969. It is a quiet, elegant pet that sheds very little. The mothers are said to be particularly attentive to their kittens.

KORAT

APPEARANCE

A strong, muscular yet slender and delicate cat of medium size, with a fairly short coat that lies close to the body. It has a heart-shaped head with a flat forehead, dark blue or lavender nose and large ears that are rounded at the tips. The large, expressive eyes are blue in the kitten but change to a striking green or green-gold as the cat matures. The medium-long tail tapers to a rounded tip. The hind legs are slightly longer than the front.

COLOR

A uniform silver-blue tipped with silver.

CHARACTERISTICS

An ancient breed originally from Thailand, where it was thought to embody prosperity and good fortune, the Korat was not brought to the United States in any quantity until the early 1960s. It is still relatively rare and should be bought only directly from breeders. It is a quiet, gentle, intelligent cat that makes an affectionate and responsive pet. Extremely playful, it can be taught to retrieve and do other small tricks.

MAINE COON CAT

APPEARANCE

A sturdy, powerful cat noted for its exceptionally large size and thick, shaggy coat of moderately long hair. It has a large, fairly wide head with a squarish muzzle and high cheekbones. The large tufted ears are set widely apart and come to a point. The oval eyes, which can be green, gold or blue, are also large and wide set. Its long, full-chested, muscular body rests on moderately long legs that have large tufted paws. The long bushy tail tapers to a blunt end.

COLOR

Any solid or mixed color.

CHARACTERISTICS

A native American cat of uncertain origin that was once thought to be part raccoon. Although the resemblance is certainly there, any direct kinship would be biologically impossible. A more likely story is that the breed developed from the mating of American cats with Turkish long-hairs brought to Maine by American seamen in the Nineteenth Century. Whatever its beginnings, it is an active, intelligent, quiet cat, particularly gentle with children. It is noted for its skill as a mouser, and its thick coat makes it especially well-suited to colder climates. The moderately long coat does not require that much grooming.

MANX

APPEARANCE

A very distinctive-looking cat with a short, arched back, exceptionally long rear legs, high, rounded rump and unusual double coat that is soft and thick underneath and glossy and somewhat harder on top. Perhaps its most distinctive physical feature is that it may be born without a tail. (Some Manx's have short, stubby tails.) The large, round head has prominent cheeks and broad, widely spaced ears that taper to a point. Somewhat rabbit-like in appearance, the Manx also walks with a characteristic rabbit-like hop and is known as a fast runner and high jumper. It has a powerful, compact, well-rounded body and a soft, unusual voice.

COLOR

All colors and mixtures including blue, white, black and red.

CHARACTERISTICS

One of the oldest breeds, the Manx probably originated on the Isle of Man in the Irish Sea, where it is still bred to this day. It is an intelligent, affectionate, playful cat with a stable, even-tempered personality. Unusually healthy and adaptable, it places very few demands upon its owner.

ORIENTAL SHORTHAIR

APPEARANCE

Closely resembling the Siamese in everything but the color and length of its coat, the Oriental Shorthair has a long wedge-shaped head with large, broadly pointed ears and slanted eyes that are either vivid blue, green or amber. The long, slender body is both graceful and muscular, with long, slim legs and a finely pointed tail.

COLOR

Solid white, black, light blue, brown, red or cream. White may be tipped with black, blue, brown, lavender or red. Also occurs in tabby patterns, tortoiseshell and patched mixtures.

CHARACTERISTICS

A hybrid developed by crossing the Siamese with a number of other breeds, this curious, intelligent animal has been found to be an affectionate, attentive pet. Although it can be somewhat temperamental and high-strung, it loves human companionship and is extremely loyal to its owner.

PERSIAN

APPEARANCE

Considered by many the most beautiful of cats for its long, fine-textured silky coat, which forms a full mane around the neck and back. Its massive head is broad and rounded, with full cheeks, large round eyes and small, wide-set tufted ears. The low-set body has large round legs and a short, full tail. The overall impression is of strength, dignity and elegance.

COLOR

Can be blue, white, red, cream or black. Usually colored uniformly, though in some varieties the hair is tipped with another shade. May also be seen with tabby, calico or tortoiseshell pattern.

The origin of the Persian is uncertain, though it most probably did come from Persia. What is certain is that it is the most popular pedigreed long-haired breed. Intelligent, affectionate and gentle, it is usually rather even-tempered. An excellent show cat, it is not really suited to households where there are young children. It does not particularly like to be held and may not go out of its way to please its owner.

REX

COLOR
Any solid or mixed color.

CHARACTERISTICS

A new breed that originated as a spontaneous mutation in England in 1950. Still quite rare and expensive, this extremely intelligent, affectionate and hardy animal makes a fine, easily trained house pet. Its coat does not shed and requires relatively little grooming. The Rex has been recommended for people who are otherwise allergic to cat hair.

APPEARANCE

A medium-sized shorthaired cat notable for its distinctive wavy coat, which can be either thick and kinky or silky and curled. It has a long, slim, muscular body with a characteristically arched back, long straight legs and long tapering tail. The small, narrow, wedge-shaped head has large, erect ears and wide-set oval eyes.

RUSSIAN BLUE

COLOR
Various uniform shades of blue—from slate blue to lavender—sometimes tipped with silver.

CHARACTERISTICS

Though its origin is uncertain, the Russian Blue may well have been brought to the West from Russia by British sailors around 1860. Hardy and active, it is at home in the outdoors but also makes a fine apartment pet—even-tempered, affectionate and attentive. It is an intelligent, loyal, unusually quiet animal.

APPEARANCE

A sleek, graceful cat with a distinctive short, dense, beaver-like coat that stands out from the body. It has a slim, lithe body with long legs and small feet. The short, wedge-shaped head has a flat forehead, long neck and large pointed ears that are set widely apart. The bright green eyes are round and widely set. The tail is medium-long and tapered.

SCOTTISH FOLD

APPEARANCE

A medium-sized shorthair with a short, well-padded body, thick coat and moderately long tapering tail. It has a well-rounded head and eyes, a short nose and prominent cheeks and whisker pads. Unlike any other breed, its ears fold forward rather than stand erect.

COLOR
Solid black, blue, red, cream or white. White may be tipped with black, red or blue. Also occurs in tabby patterns, tortoiseshell and calico mixtures.

CHARACTERISTICS

One of the newest breeds, the Scottish Fold first occurred in Scotland as a mutation. Since its original appearance, it has been carefully bred to preserve its uniquely folded ears.

SIAMESE

APPEARANCE

A strikingly handsome shorthair with a distinctively marked fine-textured, glossy coat. Its long, wedge-shaped head has large, broad, pointed ears and vivid blue slanted eyes. The long, slender body is both graceful and muscular, with long slim legs and a long tapered tail that is sometimes kinked at the end.

COLOR
Cream gradually darkening to light brown, marked with seal brown points on the face, ears, legs, feet and tail.

Bluish-white marked with blue points. Ivory marked with chocolate points. Glacial white marked with lilac points. Kittens are always born white, and develop their coat and point colors at about three months.

CHARACTERISTICS

Probably the most popular of pedigreed breeds, originating in Thailand and first brought to England and the United States in the latter part of the Nineteenth Century. Prized as a show cat, it also makes an affectionate, attentive pet. It loves human companionship and, despite some reputation for being temperamental and high-strung, is extremely loyal to its owner. Curious, intelligent and easily trained, it can be taught to perform small tricks like a dog. The Siamese is a particularly talkative cat, and some people find its loud, unusual voice rather annoying.

SOMALI

APPEARANCE

Except for its extremely soft, finely textured medium-length coat, the Somali closely resembles the Abyssinian. It is a medium to large cat with a softly rounded wedge-shaped head and large, moderately pointed ears. The large almond-shaped eyes are either vivid green or gold. The graceful body is sleek, slender and muscular, with a slightly arched back that makes the cat look as if it were about to spring. The tail is thick at the base and somewhat tapering.

COLOR

Ruddy brown with darker shading or black on the tips of the ears and along the spine and tail. Deep red with dark brown ticking that emerges slowly as the kitten matures.

CHARACTERISTICS

A gentle, affectionate cat that makes a lively, even-tempered, devoted pet. Unusually intelligent and active, it dislikes being confined too closely.

TURKISH ANGORA

APPEARANCE

A fine-boned, long-legged medium-sized cat with fairly long, fine silky hair that forms a ruff around its neck. It has a pointed head that tapers toward the rounded jaws and long tufted ears that are wide at the base and come to a point. Its large round or almond-shaped amber eyes are unusually expressive. White cats may have blue eyes or one blue and the other amber. The rump of its long, graceful body is slightly higher than the front. Its long tail tapers toward the end and is carried horizontally over the body when the cat is in motion.

COLOR

White, black or blue. White may be solid or tipped with black or blue. Tabby striping, calico or white with patches of blue, black or red are also found.

CHARACTERISTICS

Named after an earlier spelling of Ankara, the capital of Turkey, this ancient long-haired breed almost lapsed into extinction because of the greater popularity of its Persian cousin. It was saved from disappearance in recent years by the Ankara Zoo, which now oversees its breeding, raising only the white-haired version. It was first brought to the United States in 1963 and only given recognition as a distinct breed in 1970. Affectionate, intelligent and playful, it makes an excellent pet and a fine show cat.

ABYSSINIAN

AMERICAN SHORTHAIR (DOMESTIC SHORTHAIR)

AMERICAN WIREHAIR

BIRMAN

BALINESE

BOMBAY

50

BRITISH SHORTHAIR

BURMESE

COLORPOINT SHORTHAIR

EGYPTIAN MAU

EXOTIC SHORTHAIR

HAVANA BROWN

HIMALAYAN

JAPANESE BOBTAIL

KORAT

53

MAINE COON CAT

MANX

ORIENTAL SHORTHAIR

54

PERSIAN

REX

RUSSIAN BLUE

SIAMESE

SCOTTISH FOLD

SOMALI

TURKISH ANGORA

RECORDS AND SUPPLIES

KITTEN GROWTH AND DEVELOPMENT

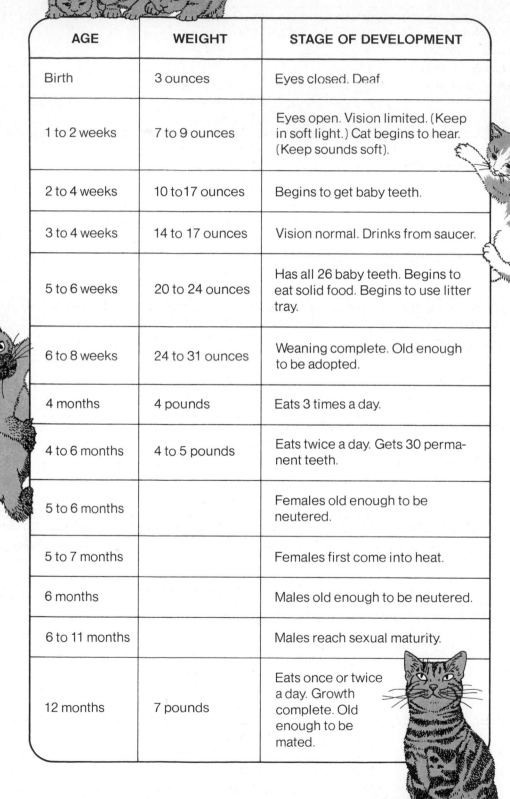

AGE	WEIGHT	STAGE OF DEVELOPMENT
Birth	3 ounces	Eyes closed. Deaf.
1 to 2 weeks	7 to 9 ounces	Eyes open. Vision limited. (Keep in soft light.) Cat begins to hear. (Keep sounds soft).
2 to 4 weeks	10 to 17 ounces	Begins to get baby teeth.
3 to 4 weeks	14 to 17 ounces	Vision normal. Drinks from saucer.
5 to 6 weeks	20 to 24 ounces	Has all 26 baby teeth. Begins to eat solid food. Begins to use litter tray.
6 to 8 weeks	24 to 31 ounces	Weaning complete. Old enough to be adopted.
4 months	4 pounds	Eats 3 times a day.
4 to 6 months	4 to 5 pounds	Eats twice a day. Gets 30 permanent teeth.
5 to 6 months		Females old enough to be neutered.
5 to 7 months		Females first come into heat.
6 months		Males old enough to be neutered.
6 to 11 months		Males reach sexual maturity.
12 months	7 pounds	Eats once or twice a day. Growth complete. Old enough to be mated.

IMMUNIZATION SCHEDULE AND RECORD

Cat's Name _____ Date of Birth _____

COMBINED FELINE DISTEMPER-FELINE RHINOTRACHEITIS-CALICI VIRUS

1st Dose (6 to 14 Weeks Old)	Date _____ Veterinarian _____
2nd Dose (After 14 Weeks)	Date _____ Veterinarian _____
Booster Shot (Annually)	Date _____ Veterinarian _____
	Date _____ Veterinarian _____
	Date _____ Veterinarian _____

RABIES

1st Dose (3 to 6 Months Old)	Date _____ Veterinarian _____
Booster Shot (Annually)	Date _____ Veterinarian _____
	Date _____ Veterinarian _____
	Date _____ Veterinarian _____

Cat's Name _____ Date of Birth _____

COMBINED FELINE DISTEMPER-FELINE RHINOTRACHEITIS-CALICI VIRUS

1st Dose (6 to 14 Weeks Old)	Date _____ Veterinarian _____
2nd Dose (After 14 Weeks)	Date _____ Veterinarian _____
Booster Shot (Annually)	Date _____ Veterinarian _____
	Date _____ Veterinarian _____
	Date _____ Veterinarian _____

RABIES

1st Dose (3 to 6 Months Old)	Date _____ Veterinarian _____
Booster Shot (Annually)	Date _____ Veterinarian _____
	Date _____ Veterinarian _____
	Date _____ Veterinarian _____

Cat's Name _____ Date of Birth _____

COMBINED FELINE DISTEMPER-FELINE RHINOTRACHEITIS-CALICI VIRUS

1st Dose (6 to 14 Weeks Old)	Date _____ Veterinarian _____
2nd Dose (After 14 Weeks)	Date _____ Veterinarian _____
Booster Shot (Annually)	Date _____ Veterinarian _____
	Date _____ Veterinarian _____
	Date _____ Veterinarian _____

RABIES

1st Dose (3 to 6 Months Old)	Date _____ Veterinarian _____
Booster Shot (Annually)	Date _____ Veterinarian _____
	Date _____ Veterinarian _____
	Date _____ Veterinarian _____

GENERAL HEALTH RECORD

Cat's Name _____ Date of Birth _____
Veterinarian: Name _____ Office Phone _____ Home Phone _____

Dates Wormed
Type _____ Date _____ Type _____ Date _____
Type _____ Date _____ Type _____ Date _____
Type _____ Date _____ Type _____ Date _____
Date Neutered _____ Veterinarian's Name _____

Present Medical Problems & Chronic Conditions _____
_____
_____

Medicines Taken Regularly _____

Special Precautions & Other Information _____

	NATURE	DATE	VETERINARIAN	PHONE
Hospitalizations				
Surgery				
Major Injuries				

Cat's Name _____ Date of Birth _____
Veterinarian: Name _____ Office Phone _____ Home Phone _____

Dates Wormed
Type _____ Date _____ Type _____ Date _____
Type _____ Date _____ Type _____ Date _____
Type _____ Date _____ Type _____ Date _____
Date Neutered _____ Veterinarian's Name _____

Present Medical Problems & Chronic Conditions _____
_____
_____

Medicines Taken Regularly _____

Special Precautions & Other Information _____

	NATURE	DATE	VETERINARIAN	PHONE
Hospitalizations				
Surgery				
Major Injuries				

Cat's Name _____ Date of Birth _____
Veterinarian: Name _____ Office Phone _____ Home Phone _____

Dates Wormed
Type _____ Date _____ Type _____ Date _____
Type _____ Date _____ Type _____ Date _____
Type _____ Date _____ Type _____ Date _____
Date Neutered _____ Veterinarian's Name _____

Present Medical Problems & Chronic Conditions _____
_____
_____

Medicines Taken Regularly _____

Special Precautions & Other Information _____

	NATURE	DATE	VETERINARIAN	PHONE
Hospitalizations				
Surgery				
Major Injuries				

STOCKING UP

☑ Absorbent Cotton Balls
☐ Activated Charcoal
☑ Adhesive Tape, 1 & 2 inches wide
☑ Antacid Liquid (Pepto-Bismol, etc.)
☐ Antibiotic Ointment
☒ Antihistamine Syrup (contained in many cough & cold preparations)
☐ Antihistamine Tablets (check for veterinarian's recommendation)
☑ Bandages, Elastic & Nonelastic
☑ Calamine Lotion
☑ Cotton Batting
☑ Cotton-Tipped Swabs
☐ Kaopectate
☑ Measuring Cup
☑ Measuring Spoons
☑ Medicinal Hydrogen Peroxide (3%), U.S.P.
☑ Nail Clipper (professional type)

☐ Nose Drops (Neosynepherine or the like)
☑ Petroleum Jelly
☑ Plastic Eyedropper or Dosing Syringe (available from veterinarian)
☑ Rectal Thermometer
☑ Rubber Gloves
☑ Rubbing Alcohol
☑ Safety Pins
☑ Scissors (with rounded edges)
☑ Sterile Gauze Pads, 2 x 4 inches
☑ Sterile Gauze Rolls, 2 & 3 inches wide
☐ "Tamed" Iodine or Other Antiseptic
☑ Tourniquet: A short, sturdy stick and a clean cloth 1 inch wide. See **BLEEDING: TOURNIQUET,** pages 122-124, before using.
☑ Tweezers or Forceps
☐ Wooden Tongue Depressors

Never give your cat aspirin or aspirin substitutes. They are highly toxic to cats.

HOME PET VET GUIDE FIRST-AID KIT

☐ Baking Soda (to eliminate litter tray odor)
☐ Cat Carrier
☐ Catnip Ball or Mouse
☐ Collar (elasticized)
☐ Comb (medium fine, smooth teeth)
☐ Food Dish (shallow, non-corrosive, easy to clean)
☐ Hard Ball (with rattle)
☐ Harness
☐ Leash

☐ Litter Pan (12" x 24" x 6", non-corrosive, easy to clean)
☐ Natural Bristle Brush
☐ Sieve (to remove solid waste from litter pan)
☐ Toys
☐ Water Dish (weighted base, deep)
☐ Wooden Scratching Post (18" to 24" high, 4" to 6" thick)

Do not let your cat play with thread or string, plastic bags, small beads or anything brittle or small enough to be swallowed.

PART TWO

THE ANATOMICAL CAT

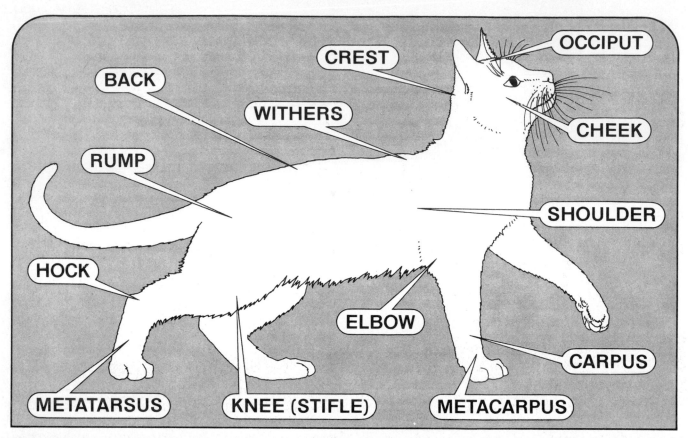

CREST
OCCIPUT
BACK
WITHERS
CHEEK
RUMP
SHOULDER
HOCK
ELBOW
CARPUS
METATARSUS
KNEE (STIFLE)
METACARPUS

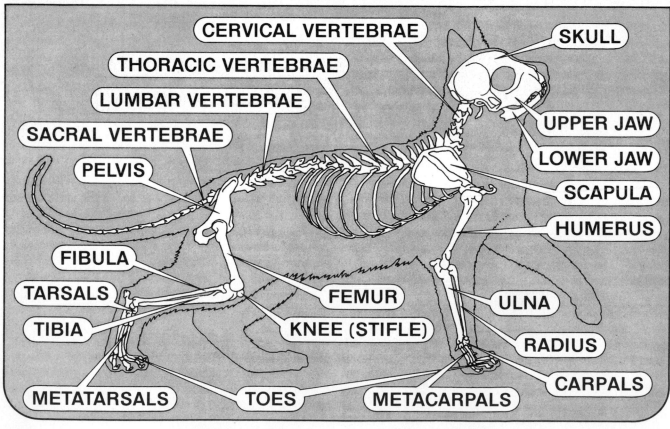

CERVICAL VERTEBRAE
SKULL
THORACIC VERTEBRAE
LUMBAR VERTEBRAE
SACRAL VERTEBRAE
UPPER JAW
PELVIS
LOWER JAW
SCAPULA
HUMERUS
FIBULA
TARSALS
FEMUR
ULNA
TIBIA
KNEE (STIFLE)
RADIUS
CARPALS
METATARSALS
TOES
METACARPALS

SYMPTOM RECOGNITION INDEX

Most of the responsibility for determining whether your cat is ill necessarily falls on you and the other members of your household. Only a small percentage of health disorders are discovered by the veterinarian during routine examinations. The rest are brought to his attention by owners who recognize, from their more or less continuous contact, that their pets aren't reacting normally and something is wrong.

Virtually any change in your cat's physical appearance or behavior can be an indication of impaired health. The symptoms presented here are the most familiar signs of the common disorders described in the two sections that follow on illnesses and health emergencies. The symptoms are arranged alphabetically. Under each symptom you will find listed the various disorders with which it is associated, along with the relevant page references.

A given symptom can usually have any number of causes. Rarely is it so unique that it is seen in one and only one illness. Most illnesses also have more than one symptom. By turning to the cited pages and comparing these other symptoms with what you observe in your cat you will be able to narrow down what is probably wrong with it and find out what to do.

As a general rule, it is best to consult your veterinarian whenever you find any symptoms of ill health in your cat, even if you are uncertain about them or they seem mild or appear only occasionally. Depending on the cause, some symptoms come on suddenly and are entirely obvious, but others may develop slowly and subtly and be only intermittent. Nor does the apparent severity of the symptom necessarily signify the seriousness of the underlying cause. Minor disorders sometimes produce dramatic symptoms, while far more serious illnesses may have symptoms that are scarcely evident. Your veterinarian would certainly prefer a false alarm to the unnecessary delay that may lead to complications or permit the disorder to worsen and perhaps even threaten the cat's life.

C

CHEWS AT SELF: See BITES, CHEWS OR LICKS AT SELF

D

DEFECATION

Constipation: See **CONSTIPATION**

Diarrhea: See **DIARRHEA**

Difficult, Painful Or Futile Attempts
- Anal Plug ... 85
- Constipation ... 86

Loss Of Bowel Control
- Convulsions & Seizures ... 141
- Idiopathic Epilepsy ... 95
- Trauma To The Spinal Column ... 96

DEHYDRATION

- Acute Enteritis ... 86
- Autoimmune Hemolytic Anemia ... 84
- Distemper ... 93
- End Stage Kidney Disease ... 105
- Pneumonia ... 100
- Pyometra (Uterine Infection) ... 106
- Rabies ... 93
- Ruptured Bladder ... 105

DEPRESSION

- Calici Virus Infection ... 92
- Diabetes Mellitus ... 95
- Distemper ... 93
- End Stage Kidney Disease ... 105
- Feline Infectious Anemia ... 93
- Heatstroke ... 159
- Pneumonia ... 100
- Pyothorax ... 101
- Rhinotracheitis ... 94
- Ruptured Bladder ... 105
- Toxoplasmosis ... 99
- Undifferentiated Respiratory Illness ... 94
- **May also signify other disorders**

DIARRHEA

- Acute Enteritis ... 86
- Coccidiosis ... 98
- Distemper ... 93
- End Stage Kidney Disease ... 105
- Foreign Objects In The Stomach ... 88
- Hookworms ... 98
- Infectious Peritonitis ... 93
- Lymphosarcoma ... 83
- Roundworms ... 99

DISORIENTATION

- Convulsions & Seizures ... 141
- Electric Shock ... 148
- Idiopathic Epilepsy ... 95
- Shock ... 170
- Trauma To The Brain ... 96
- **May also signify other disorders**

DISTRESS

- Diaphragmatic Hernia ... 91
- Urolithiasis (Urinary Calculi) ... 106
- **May also signify other disorders**

DIZZINESS

- Vestibular Disease ... 96
- **May also signify other disorders**

DROOLING

- Foreign Objects In The Esophagus ... 85
- Rabies ... 93
- Rhinotracheitis ... 94
- Undifferentiated Respiratory Illness ... 94

E

EARS

Bald Spots
- Ear Mites ... 97
- Head Mange ... 103

Crumbly Wax
- Ear Mites ... 97

Dark Material Inside
- Ear Mites ... 97

Discharge
- Otitis Externa ... 88

Foul Odor
- Otitis Externa ... 88

Infection
- Otitis Externa ... 88

Inflammation
- Otitis Externa ... 88

Pain
- Hematoma ... 88
- Otitis Externa ... 88

F

INTERNAL ORGANS EXPOSED

QUILLS EMBEDDED IN BODY

RESISTS EFFORTS TO NURSE

RESTLESSNESS

SALIVATION (PROFUSE OR THICK)

SCABS

SCRATCHES AT SELF

SEIZURES

ROAMING

ROLLS ON GROUND

RUNNING (AIMLESS OR FRENZIED)

SEMICONSCIOUSNESS

SHOCK

SKIN

T

TAIL IS LIMP

TEETH

TEMPERATURE: See FEVER

THIRST (EXCESSIVE)

TOES ARE WIDESPREAD & SPLAYED OUTWARD

(W)

WALKING DIFFICULTY

WEAKNESS

WEIGHT LOSS

WHEEZING

WORMS

WOUNDS

ILLNESSES AND DISORDERS

This section describes the illnesses and disorders that are most likely to beset your cat. Each is discussed in terms of its common symptoms, underlying cause and, most importantly, what you as the cat's owner should do about it. Special precautions and recommendations for prevention are also indicated whenever they are appropriate. For infectious diseases, you will also find information about incubation, communicability and duration.

The section is designed to be used as a reference guide to help you understand and cope with conditions that may impair your pet's normal good health. It is not a substitute for a veterinarian, though in those rare situations where veterinary care is inaccessible or delayed, it may indeed enable you to preserve your cat's life until professional help can be obtained.

Keep in mind that a cat afflicted by a given disorder may show some, all or none of the listed symptoms. And to stress an earlier point, it is usually best to tell your veterinarian about any indication of illness, no matter how minor it may seem. By the same token, if your cat is hit by a car or subjected to some other severe blow, it should be examined by the vet even if no symptoms are evident.

Cats are hardy animals, and with proper veterinary treatment and home care they usually recover from most illnesses. Sometimes, however, they do not. The responsibilities of ownership are never quite so troublesome as when a cherished pet is painfully debilitated by a serious illness and has little or no chance of recovering. Some owners deal with the problem by letting nature take its course. Others make the difficult decision to end the pet's suffering through euthanasia and submit it to a painless and peaceful death.

Should you ever have to confront this disturbing choice, your veterinarian will be able to give you some approximate idea about the cat's chances for getting better as well as how long it will take and what it will cost. He can provide you with the best available information and advice, but of course the ultimate decision has to rest with you yourself. If it seems best to have euthanasia performed on your cat, the vet can give it a quick, painless death through an overdose of anesthetic. He can also arrange to dispose of the remains. In some communities, it is possible to have a cat cremated and buried in a pet cemetary.

CANCER

LYMPHOSARCOMA

SYMPTOMS

LYMPHOSARCOMA OCCURS IN 3 FORMS: THYMIC, ALIMENTARY AND MULTICENTRIC. EACH FORM AFFECTS A DIFFERENT AREA OF THE BODY AND HAS DIFFERENT SYMPTOMS. SYMPTOMS OF THYMIC LYMPHOSARCOMA (AFFECTS THE CHEST): **Severe labored breathing. Coughing. Vomiting. Fluid-filled chest. The cat's abdomen rises and falls when it tries to breathe. The lips, tongue, gums and inner linings of the eyelids become progressively more blue.** SYMPTOMS OF ALIMENTARY LYMPHOSARCOMA (AFFECTS THE DIGESTIVE SYSTEM): **Chronic diarrhea or constipation. Loss of appetite. Swollen or painful stomach. The cat keeps its back arched.** SYMPTOMS OF MULTICENTRIC LYMPHOSARCOMA (AFFECTS MANY DIFFERENT PARTS OF THE BODY INCLUDING THE KIDNEYS, LIVER, SPLEEN, LUNGS AND BRAIN): **Vary widely according to location but can include: An ulcer in the mouth that does not heal. Loss of appetite. Weight loss.** A common cancerous tumor of the lymph nodes caused by the feline leukemia virus. Results in a dramatic overproduction of lymphocytes, a type of blood cell important in fighting infection.

WHAT TO DO

• Consult your veterinarian. Early treatment is important.
• The virus can spread to other cats in the household.

MAMMARY TUMORS

SYMPTOMS

Hard, knot-like swellings can be clearly seen and felt within the breast. As these tumors grow—and they can become very large—the skin covering them becomes thin, then ulcerated and bloody. The cat shows pain and chews or licks at the affected area. The tumors can be either benign or malignant. Usually occur in female cats. Most common in cats that develop false pregnancy. The precise cause is unknown, although related to the female hormone.

WHAT TO DO

• **Consult your veterinarian. Early treatment is important.** Malignant tumors can spread and affect other areas of the body. Surgery is usually required. To reduce occurrence in the cat's other breasts, spaying is often recommended.

• Can be effectively prevented by neutering the cat when it is about 6 months old.

SKIN CANCER

SYMPTOMS

A solid lump can be clearly seen and felt on the skin. If left untreated, the lump continues to grow. May be benign or malignant. Usually seen in older cats.

WHAT TO DO

• **Consult your veterinarian. Early treatment is important.** Malignant skin cancer can spread and affect other areas of the body.

SQUAMOUS CELL CARCINOMA

SYMPTOMS

A sore or ulcer that does not heal on the mouth, lips, tongue, eye, eyelid or elsewhere on the body where mucous membranes meet the skin. The affected area grows in size, becomes angry, inflamed and rough, and emits a foul odor. In later stages, it may increase in thickness and take on a fatty, cauliflower-like appearance. A very serious fast-growing cancer.

WHAT TO DO

• **Consult your veterinarian. Early care is essential.** Squamous cell cancer tends to spread and affect regional lymph nodes and other areas. Surgery is required.

• After treatment an affected animal should be watched closely for symptoms of recurrence.

CIRCULATORY DISORDERS

ANEMIA

SYMPTOMS

Progressive weakness and fatigue. In advanced cases, the mucous membranes of the gums, mouth and inner linings of the eyelids look pale and whitish rather than a normal healthy pink. A consequence of any condition that results in an inadequate supply of circulating red blood cells. Various causes include reduced production of red blood cells (inadequate diet, leukemia in the bone marrow, etc.), increased rate of destruction of red blood cells (poisoning, diseases such as feline infectious anemia, etc.) and blood loss (trauma, acute hemorrhage, parasites, etc.).

WHAT TO DO

• **Consult your veterinarian.**

AORTIC THROMBOSIS (EMBOLISM)

SYMPTOMS

Very sudden paralysis of the muscles in the hind legs. The cat may cry out in pain, especially when its legs are squeezed. The legs are cold to the touch, and no pulse can be felt. The calf muscles contract and become very hard. The cat's bowel and bladder functions remain normal. Commonly occurs as a result of heart muscle disease when a piece of a clot breaks off from inside the heart and becomes lodged in the blood vessels going to the hind legs, cutting off their blood supply. If the piece of clot lodges elsewhere, other parts of the body will be affected.

WHAT TO DO

• **Consult your veterinarian. Prompt treatment is important.**

AUTOIMMUNE HEMOLYTIC ANEMIA

SYMPTOMS

A sudden or gradually developing paleness of the tongue, gums and inner linings of the eyelids. Weakness. Loss of appetite. Dehydration. Caused by the production of antibodies that destroy the red blood cells. Can develop slowly or rapidly. May recur after treatment.

WHAT TO DO

• **Consult your veterinarian. Early treatment is important.**

HEART MURMUR

SYMPTOMS

IN OLDER ANIMALS: Coughing. Difficulty breathing. Fluid-filled "potbelly." IN KITTENS: May be without apparent symptoms, or a "hum" or "purr" may be felt in the chest. A result of any interference with the normal flow of blood through the heart. Can be present from birth or acquired with age. In kittens, can be caused by the failure of fetal heart openings to close fully when the animal is born or by defects in the shape of the heart or its valves.

WHAT TO DO

• **Consult your veterinarian.**

HEART MUSCLE DISEASE (IDIOPATHIC CARDIOMYOPATHY)

SYMPTOMS

Fluid-filled "potbelly." Loss of appetite. Gradual weight loss. The cat may or may not have difficulty breathing. The condition slowly worsens. In advanced cases: Weight loss may become extreme within just a few weeks. Quickly worsening breathing difficulties. Coughing. A common disease of unknown cause in which the heart muscle fails to function properly and the heart becomes enlarged. May affect one or both sides of the heart. Can affect cats of any age.

WHAT TO DO

• **Consult your veterinarian. Early care is essential.** Ongoing medication is usually required. The medication can improve the functioning of the heart and slow the progress of the disease, but cannot effect a complete cure.

• Continue to observe an affected cat for the onset of **AORTIC THROMBOSIS;** see above.

DIGESTIVE DISORDERS: ANUS

ANAL PLUG

SYMPTOMS

Accumulated stool and matted hair around the anus, which blocks defecation. Pain in the affected area. The cat scoots or rubs its rear end on the ground. Straining during futile attempts to defecate. Foul odor. The skin under the matted hair is irritated and inflamed. A common condition in long-haired kittens and cats.

WHAT TO DO

• Consult your veterinarian.
• **For home care:** Restrain the cat; see **RESTRAINTS**, page 177. Gently cut away the hair that holds the plug against the skin and remove the mass. Clean the area with hand soap and warm water.
• To prevent recurrence, keep the hair around the anus trimmed short and check the area frequently.

ANAL SAC ABSCESS

SYMPTOMS

Hot, painful swelling to the sides of the anus or just below it. The cat may rub, lick or bite at the area. The abscess may eventually open a small hole, through which pus and blood may drain. Caused by an infection of the anal sacs. These sacs are normally emptied of their secretions by the pressure of the cat defecating. For unknown reasons, the secretions can thicken and block the openings in the sacs, causing inflammation and abscess.

WHAT TO DO

• **Consult your veterinarian.** Surgery is usually required.

• As a prevention, examine your cat's anus regularly and have the veterinarian clear the anal sacs if necessary.

RECTAL PROLAPSE

SYMPTOMS

A small or large cylindrical red mass protrudes from the anus. It is very inflamed and may also be bloody. Results from a long period of straining to defecate. Common causes include chronic constipation, urinary obstruction or infection, tumor and birth difficulties. Sometimes caused in kittens by severe diarrhea.

WHAT TO DO

• **Consult your veterinarian. Early care is important.**
• If a vet isn't immediately available, apply cold moistened cloth compresses against the exposed tissue. This will prevent further exposure, hold down the swelling, keep the tissue clean and prevent it from drying out.
• As a precaution, tell your veterinarian if your cat strains frequently while defecating.

DIGESTIVE DISORDERS: ESOPHAGUS

FOREIGN OBJECTS IN THE ESOPHAGUS

SYMPTOMS

Drooling and persistent gulping because of bones, fishhooks, threaded needles, etc. that have been swallowed and become stuck in the esophagus. The cat tries to vomit or does vomit. The vomit contains some blood. Anxiety. If there is a partial obstruction, the appetite may be unaffected, or the cat may be able to drink liquids but attempts to throw up solids.

WHAT TO DO

• **Consult your veterinarian. Early treatment is essential** to prevent damage to the esophagus or pneumonia from inhaled food caught behind the object. **Do not** give the cat food or water.
• As a prevention: Try to keep your cat from playing with string or small objects that can be swallowed. Never feed it bones or fish that contains bones.

DIGESTIVE DISORDERS: INTESTINES

ACUTE ENTERITIS

SYMPTOMS

Diarrhea, with or without blood. Often follows bouts of vomiting within 24 hours. The hair around the anus may become dirty, matted and foul-smelling. An acute inflammation of the intestines from various causes including foreign material, bacteria, virus infection, toxic agents and chemicals. Can lead to dehydration if severe or prolonged. Bloody diarrhea can be serious because of the possibility of substantial blood loss. The diarrhea may not be noticed unless the cat has an accident inside the house.

WHAT TO DO

• **Consult your veterinarian.**

• **For home care:** see **DIARRHEA,** page 142.

CONSTIPATION

SYMPTOMS

The cat makes frequent trips to the litter box without being able to defecate. It may remain in a defecating position for long periods.

WHAT TO DO

• **Consult your veterinarian** if the constipation lasts more than 2 days.

• The symptoms of constipation are similar to those of **UROLITHIASIS,** see page 106, a much more serious illness. Consult your veterinarian immediately if you are not absolutely certain the cat is urinating.

• If your cat has a history of constipation, give it applesauce at every meal along with its other food, or mix 1 teaspoon of vegetable oil in its food 3 or 4 times a week.

INTESTINAL OBSTRUCTION AND INTUSSUSCEPTION

SYMPTOMS

Vomiting. Loss of appetite. Swollen or painful stomach. Arching of the back. The cat passes bloody mucus or dark, tar-like stool. A condition in which the intestinal tract is partially or totally blocked, slowing or stopping the normal passage of food. Most commonly caused by tumors or foreign objects such as stones, bones and hair balls. Occasionally, a section of intestine may begin to fold like a telescope, producing an obstruction called "intussusception." Usually acute, but can be chronic or intermittent. Severity is determined by the degree of the blockage and where it occurs.

WHAT TO DO

• **Consult your veterinarian. Early treatment is important.**

• Withhold food and water until your vet sees the cat.

DIGESTIVE DISORDERS: MOUTH

FOREIGN OBJECTS IN THE MOUTH

SYMPTOMS

Violent pawing at the face. Rubbing the mouth along the floor. The cat may not be able to close its mouth. Profuse salivation. Futile attempts to dislodge the object with violent tongue movements. Commonly caused by biting down on sticks, pieces of bone or plastic, threaded needles, fishhooks, etc. that then become stuck between two teeth or across the roof of the mouth. Usually, but not always, involves the upper teeth.

WHAT TO DO

• **Consult your veterinarian** if the cat has a needle or fishhook stuck in its mouth.

• For other objects: Restrain the cat; see **RESTRAINTS,** page 177. Open its mouth and carefully check the upper and lower teeth and the roof of the mouth. Grasp the object firmly with pliers or your fingers, and gently remove it. (Usually, no additional care is required. Small cuts in the mouth heal quickly.)

• If you can't locate a foreign object and the symptoms persist, consult your veterinarian.

INFLAMMATION AND ULCERS

SYMPTOMS

Red, angry areas on the lips, tongue or inside the cheeks. Profuse salivation. Unwillingness to eat. Pain. The cat may paw at its mouth. May also include symptoms of respiratory illness such as sneezing, coughing or discharge from the nose or eyes. Common causes include irritation from tooth infection, respiratory virus, calici virus, burns from chemicals and biting an electrical cord.

WHAT TO DO

• Consult your veterinarian.

• To avoid further inflammation, give the cat only bland food and drink served at room temperature.

• Watch the cat closely. Consult your veterinarian again if the inflammation and ulcers haven't disappeared within 5-10 days or if respiratory symptoms develop.

PYORRHEA (TOOTH INFECTION)

SYMPTOMS

Inflammation and infection of the gums around the teeth. Bleeding. Lost or loose teeth. Foul breath. Loss of appetite. Ulcers on the lining of the cheek near the affected teeth. Cavity-like pitting of the teeth at the gum line. The gums are sensitive to the touch. A result of tooth tartar and gingivitis.

WHAT TO DO

• Consult your veterinarian. Early treatment is important to prevent tooth loss, weakened bone structure, more serious infection and systemic damage from chronic infection in the mouth.

RETENTION OF KITTEN (DECIDUOUS) TEETH

SYMPTOMS

The small kitten teeth do not fall out as the larger permanent teeth grow in but remain in the mouth next to or behind the permanent teeth. Normally, kitten teeth are replaced before the cat is 6 months old.

WHAT TO DO

• Consult your veterinarian. If not removed, the kitten teeth may distort the shape or location of the permanent teeth or cause the jaw to close improperly.

TOOTH TARTAR AND GINGIVITIS

SYMPTOMS

Tan or brown discoloration of the teeth, starting at the gum line and progressing under the gums and over the teeth. Cavity-like pitting of the teeth at the gum line. The gums are sensitive to the touch. Loss of appetite. Inflammation or infection of the gums around the teeth. Receding gums. Lost or loose teeth. Foul breath.

WHAT TO DO

• Consult your veterinarian.

• If necessary, have your vet clean your cat's teeth once a year. This will remove accumulated tartar and reduce the likelihood of inflammation, infection and abscess.

• Some cats accumulate tartar quickly. You can slow this accumulation between regular visits to the veterinarian by vigorous weekly brushings with a moist toothbrush and occasionally feeding your cat dry, crunchy cat food.

UPPER P4 SYNDROME

SYMPTOMS

An infection of one of the fourth premolars (P4), the large upper teeth directly under the cat's sinuses. (The infected tooth may appear normal.) The cheekbone directly under the eye protrudes from the pus that fills the sinus cavity and distorts the cat's face. In advanced cases, a small opening develops under the eye and pus drains down the cat's cheek.

WHAT TO DO

• Consult your veterinarian. Early treatment is important.

DIGESTIVE DISORDERS: STOMACH

ACUTE GASTRITIS

SYMPTOMS
A sudden, brief episode of vomiting, which may or may not recur. May be caused by eating spoiled food or foreign materials, bacteria, virus infection, toxic agents, poison or chemicals. A common condition.

WHAT TO DO
• Treat the cat for **VOMITING**; see page 174.

FOREIGN OBJECTS IN THE STOMACH

SYMPTOMS
Sudden brief episodes of vomiting or diarrhea. The vomit or diarrhea may contain blood or hair. Caused when indigestible objects such as bones, stones or pieces of metal are swallowed and remain in the stomach. Can also result from the accumulation of swallowed hair into a hair ball. May be recurrent in some cats.

WHAT TO DO
• **Consult your veterinarian. Early treatment is essential** to prevent the object from passing into the intestines, where it may present a more serious problem. May require surgical removal. Some foreign objects, including hair balls, can be passed with the use of prescribed laxatives.

EARS

HEMATOMA

SYMPTOMS
A large or small painful soft swelling on the ear flap. Caused by accumulated blood from a broken blood vessel in the cartilage of the flap. Often a result of head shaking and ear scratching due to otitis externa or ear mites.

WHAT TO DO
• **Consult your veterinarian.** Failure to treat will cause a knotting and constriction of the cartilage and result in a permanently disfigured "cauliflower" ear. Treatment involves draining the blood from the ear flap and binding it tightly to prevent disfiguration. May recur if the underlying cause is not eliminated.

• Always check with your veterinarian if your cat scratches its ears frequently or shows other symptoms of **OTITIS EXTERNA**; see below.

• As a prevention, clean your cat's ears regularly to keep them free of accumulated wax and debris; see **CLEANING THE CAT'S EARS**, page 31.

OTITIS EXTERNA

SYMPTOMS
Shaking the head or tipping it to one side. Scratching at ears. Discomfort or pain when the ear or ear flap is touched. The skin in the ear canal is thickened, red and angry and may ooze serum or pus. Foul odor. A common inflammation of the ear canal due to irritation caused by **EAR MITES**, page 97, or accumulated wax and debris. The inflammation allows various bacteria to infect the area. Can progress to ulceration of parts of the ear canal.

WHAT TO DO
• **Consult your veterinarian** if there are signs of infection. You may have to administer long-term care to keep the cat's ears clean and medicated until they heal.

• You may be able to treat a less serious case yourself by keeping your cat's ears clean; see **CLEANING THE CAT'S EARS**, page 31.

• To prevent otitis, clean your cat's ears regularly to keep them free of accumulated wax and debris.

• Prolonged scratching and head shaking can result in **HEMATOMA**; see above.

EYES

CATARACTS

SYMPTOMS

The pupil of the eye becomes whitish-blue, then gradually turns milky white and opaque as the disease progresses. Indications of reduced vision, particularly in dim light. May affect one or both eyes. Can occur at any age. (Older cats sometimes have a whitish-blue haze in their eyes that resembles cataracts but does not affect their vision.)

WHAT TO DO

• **Consult your veterinarian.** Surgery is usually recommended when vision is lost. An affected cat may also have other eye diseases or diabetes mellitus.

• A cat that has undergone cataract surgery will have less than normal vision but will be able to function quite well. You should, however, carefully plan its environment to protect it from new dangers arising from its partial loss of sight.

CONJUNCTIVITIS

SYMPTOMS

Pink or red inflamed eyes, eyeballs or inner linings of the eyelids. Squinting and sensitivity to light. Discomfort. Possible pus-like discharge. Possible exposure of the opaque third eyelid, which is normally not seen. May be accompanied by fever. Common causes include direct irritation, injury and infectious diseases. Can affect one or both eyes. If seen in one eye, it is most likely a local problem from irritation or injury. If seen in both eyes, it might be a local problem or an indication of a serious systemic illness such as rhinotracheitis, calici virus or undifferentiated respiratory illness.

WHAT TO DO

• **Consult your veterinarian. Prompt treatment is important.**

• Keep the eyes clean and free of debris; see **CLEANING THE CAT'S EYES,** page 32.

• Depending on the cause, conjunctivitis can sometimes be contagious through direct contact. An affected cat should be isolated until it has been properly diagnosed.

• Should the opaque third eyelid come up to protect the injured eye, **do not** try to remove it or otherwise interfere with it.

CORNEAL ULCER

SYMPTOMS

Extreme pain in the eye. Tearing. Squinting and sensitivity to light. The surface of the eyeball is roughened and dished out rather than smooth and mirror-like. Caused by a loss of substance of the transparent membrane covering the eye. May result from chronic irritation, foreign bodies caught under the eyelid, chronic conjunctivitis or keratitis. A serious problem that can lead to blindness if not treated. In severe cases, the ulcers may actually penetrate the cornea, resulting in extreme damage that threatens the eyeball.

WHAT TO DO

• **Consult your veterinarian. Early care is important.** May require extended treatment or surgery.

• Early treatment of eye irritation and **CONJUNCTIVITIS,** see above, can help prevent this condition.

• As a further precaution, examine your cat's eyes regularly.

EPIPHORA

SYMPTOMS

Dark tear staining of the fur and skin in the corner of the eye closest to the nose. Caused by an excess production of tears resulting from an irritation of the eye or an obstruction or blockage of the tear duct.

WHAT TO DO

• Consult your veterinarian.

• **For home care:** Keep your cat's eyes clean; see **CLEANING THE CAT'S EYES,** page 32. Medicinal hydrogen peroxide applied with a cotton-tipped swab can be used to bleach out stains caused by tears on the hair below the eye. (Take care not to get hydrogen peroxide in the cat's eyes.)

EXPOSURE OF THE THIRD EYELID

SYMPTOMS

An opaque film rises from the lower corner of the eye nearest the nose and covers some portion of the eyeball. The eyeball may seem to have moved upward out of its normal position. The third eyelid serves as a protective device for the eye and is normally not seen unless the eye is injured, irritated or inflamed, or the cat is suffering from depression or an upper respiratory illness. Often occurs with conjunctivitis. If seen in both eyes, may be a symptom of upper respiratory illness or depression.

WHAT TO DO

• **Consult your veterinarian.**
• **Do not** try to remove the third eyelid or otherwise interfere with it.
• As a prevention, keep the eyes clean and free of debris; see **CLEANING THE CAT'S EYES,** page 32.

FOLDED EYELID

SYMPTOMS

IF THE EDGE OF THE EYELID FOLDS INWARD TOWARD THE EYEBALL: Squinting and sensitivity to light. Possible exposure of the third eyelid, which is not normally seen. IF THE EDGE OF THE EYELID FOLDS OUTWARD AWAY FROM THE EYEBALL: The eye is chronically red and angry. Conjunctivitis, with or without pus in the sac formed by the eyelid. May result from a birth defect or can occur at some later time. May affect either the upper or lower lid in one or both eyes. An outward-folding eyelid more often affects the lower lid.

WHAT TO DO

• **Consult your veterinarian.** Can progress to **KERATITIS,** see below, or **CORNEAL ULCER,** page 89. Surgery is usually required.
• Should the opaque third eyelid come up to protect the injured eye, **do not** try to remove it or otherwise interfere with it.

GLAUCOMA

SYMPTOMS

Any signs of decreased vision, particularly in dim light. Obvious enlargement of the eyeball, with or without red and enlarged surface blood vessels. The eye appears hazy. When felt through the eyelid, the eye seems harder than normal. Caused by increased pressure within the eye. May be a result of increased production of the normal fluid in the eye or some interference with the normal flow of excess fluid from the eye. Usually develops slowly over a long period of time, but may appear quite suddenly. Some vision may be permanently lost before the disease is discovered. May affect one or both eyes.

WHAT TO DO

• **Consult your veterinarian. Early treatment is important.** Surgery may be recommended.

KERATITIS

SYMPTOMS

Tearing. Pain. Squinting and sensitivity to light. The cornea is covered by a blue haze. Exposure of the third eyelid, which is not normally seen. The result of an inflammation of the cornea, the transparent covering of the eye. May affect one or both eyes. Common causes include direct irritation of the cornea, infectious diseases and injury.

WHAT TO DO

• **Consult your veterinarian. Early treatment is important.** If not treated promptly and effectively, may lead to a more serious eye condition such as **CORNEAL ULCER,** page 89, or the deposit of black pigment on the cornea, which produces partial or total blindness.
• Keep the eyes clean and free of debris; see **CLEANING THE CAT'S EYES,** page 32.
• Should the third eyelid come up to protect the injured eye, **do not** try to remove it or otherwise interfere with it.

RETINAL DISEASES

SYMPTOMS

Sudden or progressive loss of vision, often beginning with loss of night vision. An impairment of the light-sensitive materials that line the inner surface of the rear of the eye. Many possible causes, including a congenital or metabolic defect, infectious disease, inflammation, injury or improper diet. Sometimes occurs in connection with infectious peritonitis, toxoplasmosis and lymphosarcoma.

WHAT TO DO
• **Consult your veterinarian.**

SUBCONJUNCTIVAL HEMORRHAGE

SYMPTOMS

A diffuse blood-red discoloration in the white of the eye. In more severe cases, the transparent membrane covering the eye may bulge out and look like a red growth. The result of ruptured small blood vessels. Most commonly caused by trauma or severe straining.

WHAT TO DO
• **Consult your veterinarian.** Only severe cases usually require treatment.
• Continue to observe an affected cat. If the condition was caused by straining, it may recur if the cause is not eliminated.

HERNIA

ABDOMINAL HERNIA

SYMPTOMS

Large swelling under the skin of the abdomen. Caused by a rupture or break in the abdominal muscles, which allows abdominal organs and other structures to protrude. Commonly the result of some trauma to the abdomen such as being hit by a car or kicked by a horse.

WHAT TO DO
• **Consult your veterinarian. Early treatment is important.** Will require surgery.

DIAPHRAGMATIC HERNIA

SYMPTOMS

Great difficulty breathing. Distress. The abdomen rises and falls as the cat tries to breathe. The cat resists being handled and may not lie down. In severe cases, the gums, tongue and inner linings of the eyelids become progressively more blue. Caused by a hole or break in the diaphragm (the muscle separating the abdomen from the chest), which allows the abdominal organs to pass into the chest. If the hole or break is large, the stomach, liver or intestines may be drawn into the chest and press on the lungs, preventing them from expanding when the cat tries to breathe. If it is small, the symptoms may not develop for several days. Usually the result of a hereditary defect in the diaphragm or a trauma. To be suspected if the cat has recently experienced an injury involving a sharp blow to the body.

WHAT TO DO
• **Consult your veterinarian. Early treatment is important.** Surgery is required.

• Try to keep the cat calm. Any excitement can cause death.

EVENTRATION

SYMPTOMS

Internal organs protrude through a surgical incision. If the skin sutures remain closed, the organs will form a large soft lump under the skin resembling a hernia and the cat will experience moderate pain. If the skin sutures are open, the internal organs will protrude completely out of the incision and the cat will experience severe pain. In both cases, the cat may lick and chew at the affected area. Can be caused by a breakdown of the tissues around the incision or by the cat biting at its stitches. Most commonly occurs in abdominal surgery and involves the intestines or other abdominal organs. Usually happens within one week of surgery.

WHAT TO DO
• **Consult your veterinarian. Early treatment is important.** Surgery is required to replace the organs and restore sutures.
• To protect exposed organs, cover them immediately with a moistened towel. Tie the towel around the cat

and keep it moistened so the exposed tissues will not become dry.

- As a prevention: Observe the incision closely after your cat has undergone surgery. Consult your veterinarian if there is swelling or the cat licks at the incision. Do not let it chew at exposed organs. This seriously complicates repair and recovery. Try to restrict exercise for 2 weeks following surgery.

INGUINAL HERNIA

SYMPTOMS

A bulge can be seen in the cat's groin, most noticeably when it stands on its hind legs. Caused by intestines and other internal structures passing through a defect in the closure of the inguinal canal, a small hole in the abdominal muscles where the nerves and arteries leave the abdomen and enter the hind legs in the groin area. The intestinal structures that come through are likely to become squeezed and twisted, cutting off the blood supply to these structures and causing them to die. A major problem that may affect one or both sides of the groin. Tends to be hereditary. May be present from birth, but often is not noticed until the cat is at least one year old. The size of the bulge varies according to what has come through, but it tends to be fairly large.

WHAT TO DO

- **Consult your veterinarian. Early treatment is important.** Usually requires surgery.

UMBILICAL HERNIA

SYMPTOMS

A "bubble" at the umbilicus (belly button) containing fatty abdominal tissue, a section of intestine or other abdominal structures. Caused when internal structures pass through an abnormal opening in the muscles that form the abdominal wall at the umbilicus. The intact outer skin holds these structures in place and prevents them from becoming exposed. If these structures become squeezed or twisted, their blood supply may be cut off and they may die. Tends to be a hereditary defect in which the abdominal wall does not close fully following birth. Most common in kittens. The hernia can vary in size but is usually small.

WHAT TO DO

- **Consult your veterinarian.** Small umbilical hernias are generally not serious and may not require treatment. Hernias that are large, constricted or contain abdominal structures should be surgically repaired.

INFECTIOUS DISEASES

CALICI VIRUS INFECTION

SYMPTOMS

Sneezing. Coughing. The eyes and nose exude pus. Conjunctivitis. Excessive salivation. Ulcerated tongue. Loss of appetite. Depression. Fever. Difficulty breathing. Can progress to pneumonia. Usually occurs only in unvaccinated cats. Most common and serious in unvaccinated kittens.

INCUBATION

1 to 21 days.

DURATION

1 to 4 weeks or longer. Can be quickly fatal to young kittens.

COMMUNICABILITY

Highly contagious to other cats. Passed by airborne droplets or by contact with infected respiratory secretions or contaminated surroundings. The virus may live for up to 10 days in a moist environment.

WHAT TO DO

- **Consult your veterinarian. Early treatment is important.** May require hospitalization.

- When the cat gets back home, it will have to be nursed with care until it fully recovers. Try to get it to eat nourishing food. Keep it warm and dry.

- If nose drops are prescribed by the vet, see **APPLYING MEDICINE TO THE NOSE,** page 197.

- Keep the cat's eyes and nose cleared of discharge; see **CLEANING THE EYES,** page 32.

- To keep the disease from infecting the other cats in your home, isolate the affected cat and have all the cats in the household vaccinated. As a further precaution, wash your hands thoroughly and change your clothes after handling the affected cat.

- Can be prevented by inoculation and annual boosters.

DISTEMPER

SYMPTOMS

Come on suddenly. Vary according to severity. May include: Severe whitish or yellow vomiting. Diarrhea. Moderate to high fever. Loss of appetite. Listlessness. Depression. The cat may hang its head over its water bowl. Dehydration. Hunched appearance. Caused by a virus. Usually occurs only in unvaccinated cats. Most common and severe in unvaccinated kittens.

INCUBATION

5 to 6 days.

DURATION

Often fatal within a week.

COMMUNICABILITY

Highly contagious to other cats. Passed by airborne droplets or by contact with infected urine, vomit or stool. For up to 6 months following infection, the cat may pass the virus in its urine. The virus can live for up to 3 months in moist indoor areas.

WHAT TO DO

- Consult your veterinarian. Early treatment is important. May require hospitalization.
- When the cat gets back home, it will have to be nursed with care until it fully recovers. Try to get it to eat nourishing food. Keep it warm and dry.
- To keep the disease from infecting the other cats in your home, be sure to wash your hands thoroughly and change your clothes after handling the affected cat or coming into direct contact with its surroundings.
- As a further precaution, isolate it from the other cats in the household and vaccinate any that haven't been inoculated within the past year.
- Can be prevented by inoculation and annual boosters.

FELINE INFECTIOUS ANEMIA

SYMPTOMS

Depression. Weakness. Pale or whitish gums, tongue or inner linings of the eyelids. Usually accompanies respiratory or other illness. Caused by a protozoan parasite that reduces the number of circulating red blood cells.

INCUBATION

About 2 weeks following infection.

DURATION

Unknown.

COMMUNICABILITY

Unknown.

WHAT TO DO

- Consult your veterinarian immediately.
- You may have to encourage the cat to keep it eating.

INFECTIOUS PERITONITIS

SYMPTOMS

Usually no apparent symptoms, but may include: Mild discharge from the eyes and nose. Loss of appetite. Gradual weight loss. Persistent fever. Diarrhea. "Potbelly." The stomach or the chest and lungs fill with fluid. Labored breathing. Pale tongue, gums and inner linings of the eyelids. Loss of balance. Convulsions. The inside of the eye appears cloudy. A chronic disease caused by a virus. May also cause death in kittens and abortion in pregnant females.

INCUBATION

1 to 2 weeks.

DURATION

Usually 1 to 4 weeks, however it may persist for months.

COMMUNICABILITY

Highly contagious. Passed by the urine of an affected cat. Cat can be infectious for years.

WHAT TO DO

- Consult your veterinarian.

RABIES

SYMPTOMS

May include: Severe changes in the cat's personality; it may show vicious, aggressive behavior, become unusually affectionate, keep itself hidden or take to roaming long distances away from home. Unusual subdued, hoarse cry. The cat's jaw hangs open and it drools saliva. (May be mistaken for a foreign object in the mouth.) The cat cannot drink and becomes dehydrated. In advanced cases, further symptoms include progressive paralysis and convulsions. A viral disease that only affects cats that have not been vaccinated against it.

INCUBATION

Varies widely. Symptoms develop anywhere from 12 days to 1 year after infection.

DURATION
Always fatal, usually within 4 days after symptoms appear.

COMMUNICABILITY
Communicable to all warm-blooded animals that have not been vaccinated against it including human beings. Passed by the saliva of an infected animal in a bite, open wound or scrape. Under certain conditions, can also be passed by airborne droplets.

WHAT TO DO
• **Consult your veterinarian immediately.**

• If you suspect rabies in your cat, confine or isolate it without handling it. Use extreme caution. Rabid cats are extremely dangerous because of the speed with which they can strike. Remember that rabies can be passed to humans.

• As a further precaution, confine any pets that have come into contact with a cat you suspect may be rabid.

• Rabies can be prevented by inoculation and annual booster shots.

RHINOTRACHEITIS

SYMPTOMS
Sneezing. Coughing. Depression. Watery or pus-like discharge from the eyes or nose. Sensitivity to light. Labored breathing. Wheezing. Fever. Depressed red ulcers on the tongue, gums or palate. Labored swallowing. Drooling. Conjunctivitis. An infectious respiratory disease caused by a virus. Usually occurs only in unvaccinated cats. Most common and serious in unvaccinated kittens.

INCUBATION
2 to 6 days.

DURATION
Varies according to severity, but usually about 2 weeks.

COMMUNICABILITY
Highly contagious to other cats. Passed by airborne droplets and by direct contact with an infected cat, contaminated surroundings or infected urine. For several months following infection, the cat may pass the virus in its urine. The virus can live for 12 hours on hard dry surfaces.

WHAT TO DO
• **Consult your veterinarian. Early treatment is important.**
• Encourage the cat to eat.
• If nose drops are prescribed by the vet, see **APPLYING MEDICINE TO THE NOSE,** page 197.
• Keep the cat's eyes and nose cleared of discharge; see **CLEANING THE EYES,** page 32.
• To keep the disease from infecting the other cats in your home, be sure to wash your hands thoroughly and change your clothes after handling the infected cat or coming into direct contact with its surroundings.
• As a further precaution, isolate it from the other cats in the household and vaccinate any that haven't been inoculated within the past year.
• Can be prevented by inoculation and annual boosters.

UNDIFFERENTIATED RESPIRATORY ILLNESS

SYMPTOMS
May include: Sneezing. Coughing. Watery or pus-like discharge from the eyes or nose. Labored breathing. Wheezing. Fever. Red ulcers on the tongue or gums. Labored swallowing. Drooling. Depression. Listlessness. Conjunctivitis. A group of various respiratory illnesses caused by a variety of different viruses. Most serious in young cats.

INCUBATION
1 week.

DURATION
Varies according to severity, but usually about 2 to 3 weeks.

COMMUNICABILITY
Highly contagious to other cats. Passed by airborne droplets and direct contact with an infected cat or contaminated surroundings.

WHAT TO DO
• **Consult your veterinarian. Early treatment is important.**
• Encourage the cat to eat.
• If nose drops are prescribed by the vet, see **APPLYING MEDICINE TO THE NOSE,** page 197.
• Keep the cat's eyes and nose cleared of discharge; see **CLEANING THE EYES,** page 32.
• If you suspect the cat is infected, isolate it from the other cats in the household.
• Be sure to wash your hands thoroughly and change your clothes after handling the affected cat or coming into direct contact with its surroundings.

METABOLIC AND HORMONAL DISORDERS

DIABETES MELLITUS

SYMPTOMS

Develop slowly and may include: Increased thirst and urination. Ravenous appetite with weight loss or no gain. Weakness. Cataracts. Advanced cases may include: Loss of appetite. Vomiting. Depression. Coma. An inadequate production of insulin by the pancreas, causing an improper use of sugar and other metabolic problems. May also result from the body's inability to utilize insulin. Most commonly occurs in male cats over 7 years old.

WHAT TO DO

- Consult your veterinarian. Early treatment is essential.
- Usually requires ongoing daily injections of insulin at home. To determine the proper dosage, you will have to test the cat's urine daily to discover the current level of glucose.
- To balance the daily doses of insulin, you will also have to regulate the cat's food intake and activity level.

ENDOCRINE ALOPECIA (HORMONAL HAIR LOSS)

SYMPTOMS

Symmetrical hair loss on both sides of the abdomen, back or hindquarters. The skin appears normal. A hormone-related condition that mostly affects altered males and spayed females. It is only rarely seen in unaltered or immature cats.

WHAT TO DO

- Consult your veterinarian.

NEUROLOGICAL DISORDERS: BRAIN

BRAIN TUMOR

SYMPTOMS

Vary according to the size and location of the tumor. May include: Personality changes. Weakness. Seizures. Paralysis. Unconsciousness. Changes in bodily functions. If the breathing or heart functions are affected the cat may die. An abnormal growth of cells within the skull that causes pressure on the brain. The underlying cause is unknown. Usually develops slowly, with symptoms progressing from mild to severe as the resulting pressure increases. Can occur at any age but most common in older cats.

WHAT TO DO

- Consult your veterinarian.

IDIOPATHIC EPILEPSY

SYMPTOMS

Vary according to severity. Mild seizures may involve just a short period of body stiffening and confusion. In more severe cases, symptoms may include: Falling. Stiffening of the body. Chomping of the jaws. Paddling motion of the legs. Jerky, uncontrollable movements, usually lasting 2 to 3 minutes. Voiding of the bladder and bowels. The cat is conscious but unresponsive. Caused by a sudden discharge of electrical impulses anywhere in the brain. The size and location of the affected area determine the kinds of symptoms seen and their severity. The underlying cause is unknown but thought to be hereditary. Not usually seen in cats under 2 or 3 years old, but can occur at any age. Symptoms can be brought on by any kind of excitement, such as a visit to the veterinarian. The disease is lifelong, although some cats have only 1 or 2 seizures a year, while others have more frequent, even daily, episodes.

WHAT TO DO

- Consult your veterinarian. Seizures can usually be controlled by anticonvulsive medications, which will allow the affected cat to lead a reasonably normal life.
- For emergency treatment: See CONVULSIONS & SEIZURES, page 141.

- Be aware that an affected cat may show fright and disorientation for 10 to 15 minutes following a seizure. **Do not** handle it during this period.

- Although convulsions are rarely fatal unless repetitive, tell your veterinarian about all of them, no matter how brief or infrequent. If left untreated, they tend to become more frequent and severe.

TRAUMA TO THE BRAIN

SYMPTOMS

Vary with severity and exact location of the injury to the brain. Symptoms may appear immediately or not until hours later. They are not usually localized in a particular part of the body. May include: Semiconsciousness or unconsciousness. Disorientation. Difficulty breathing or moving parts of the body. Bleeding from the ears, nose or mouth. Convulsions. Wild, uncontrollable movement. Frenzied, aimless running. A sudden injury to the brain caused by a severe blow to the head, car accident or collision with a fixed object. The symptoms are commonly produced by a depressed fracture of the skull or bleeding within the skull which causes pressure on the brain.

WHAT TO DO

- **Consult your veterinarian. Early treatment is important.**

- As a precaution, if your cat is hit by a car or subjected to a serious head blow, try to keep it calm and still until seen by the veterinarian.

VESTIBULAR DISEASE

SYMPTOMS

Sudden severe twisting of the head and neck to one side. Apparent dizziness. The cat may lose its balance, fall down and roll in one direction like a barrel. Rapid eye movements. Vomiting. An inflammation of the nerves, inner ear or areas of the brain that control the sense of body position. Very often mistaken for a stroke.

WHAT TO DO

- **Consult your veterinarian. Early treatment is important.** Some cats are left with a slight permanent head tilt but still function normally.

NEUROLOGICAL DISORDERS: SPINE

TRAUMA TO THE SPINAL COLUMN

SYMPTOMS

Vary according to severity and the exact location of the spinal injury. Symptoms usually affect parts of the body behind the point of the injury. May include: Pain. Weak and wobbly rear legs. Muscle spasms in the rear legs. Partial or total paralysis of the rear legs. Limp tail. Loss of sensation. Depression of the backbone at the point of injury. In severe cases, symptoms may also include: Stiff, fully extended front legs. Loss of bowel and bladder control. Commonly caused by a car accident or a fall from a great height. Usually involves a fracture or dislocation of the spinal bones and pressure against the spine.

WHAT TO DO

- **Consult your veterinarian. Early treatment is important.** Depending upon the severity, the symptoms may be temporary or permanent. Recovery is slow.

- Transport the cat to the vet with a minimum of movement. See **TRANSPORTING A CAT,** page 172.

- Until you transport it, keep the cat as immobile as possible, preferably in a cage or box. Unnecessary movement can worsen the injuries.

PARASITES: EXTERNAL

EAR MITES

APPEARANCE
Virtually invisible to the naked eye.

SYMPTOMS
Dark soil-like material, scabs or crumbly wax on the inside of the ear. The cat may or may not scratch at its ears or shake its head with agitation. In an advanced case, the cat may develop bald spots, reddening or infection inside its ear.

WHAT TO DO
• Treat the cat at home with commercial ear mite medication made especially for use on cats. See **APPLYING MEDICINE TO THE EARS,** page 191. After each application, vigorously massage the outside of the ear, then clean the inside carefully with a cotton-tipped swab. See **CLEANING THE CAT'S EARS,** page 31. Continue applications until the cat has recovered. May require extended treatment.

• **Consult your veterinarian** if the cat does not respond to treatment.

• Ear mites are easily passed to dogs and other cats. As a precaution, treat the unaffected animals in your home once a week until the affected cat is cured. (Treat a dog with medication made especially for use on dogs.)

• To help prevent ear mites, treat your cat regularly over its entire body with mite, flea or tick insecticide made especially for use on cats. Also apply the insecticide to the cat's bedding and the other areas it frequents.

FLEAS

APPEARANCE
Small, dark, flat, hard-shelled and wingless. Quick-moving. When seen off the cat, they jump rather than crawl. Dark specks of flea excrement on the cat's fur will turn red when moistened with water.

SYMPTOMS
The cat may or may not scratch at itself. Bald or reddened areas may indicate flea allergy. In advanced cases, the cat may chew at the infested areas.

WHAT TO DO
• Treat the cat at home with flea powder, collar, bath or spray made especially for use on cats. Follow the accompanying directions carefully. If you give the cat a flea collar, **do not** also treat it with a flea bath. Using both can cause serious poisoning. Always restrain the cat before administering treatment. See **RESTRAINTS,** page 177.

• Discard or thoroughly wash the cat's bedding, and make sure to keep the bedding clean.

• For 4 to 6 weeks following treatment (or as long as necessary), apply cat flea powder weekly to the cat's bedding and the other areas it frequents.

• **Consult your veterinarian** if the cat does not respond to treatment or if it shows an allergic reaction to fleas. See **FLEA ALLERGY DERMATITIS,** page 103.

• As a precaution, treat all cats and dogs in the household for fleas. Fleas can be passed to other pets and humans and can cause anemia in very young kittens and puppies. Only use cat medication for cats and dog medication for dogs.

• If repeated treatment of animals and animal areas does not end the problem, you may have to decontaminate the entire house, particularly if it is winter.

LICE

APPEARANCE
Extremely small, white, flat and wingless. Move by crawling. Eggs attached to the cat's hairs may appear silver or white.

SYMPTOMS
Scratching. Biting at self. Restlessness.

WHAT TO DO
• Treat the cat at home with parasite bath or powder made especially for use on cats. Follow the accompanying directions carefully. Always restrain the cat before administering treatment. See **RESTRAINTS,** page 177.

• **Consult your veterinarian** if the cat does not respond to treatment.

• Lice can be passed to other cats and to dogs. They most commonly infest pets living on a farm. As a precaution, treat the unaffected animals in your home until the affected cat is cured. (Treat a dog with medication made especially for use on dogs.)

MAGGOTS

APPEARANCE
Light yellow carrot-shaped worms about 1/2 inch long. Worm-like movement. May be mistaken for tapeworms. Maggots are the hatched larvae of flies that have laid their eggs in dead or decaying tissue.

SYMPTOMS
Flies seen around open wounds or dead tissue, partic- ularly around the anus. Maggots crawl in and under the cat's flesh.

WHAT TO DO
- **Consult your veterinarian.**
- As a precaution, try to keep flies away from old or weakened cats, particularly in warm weather.

TICKS

APPEARANCE
Relatively large, dark, flat or grape-like, and wingless. Move by crawling. The legs can be seen if you move the tick with your finger. Only the mouth is embedded below the surface, not the entire body. The body looks like a mole or wart on the skin.

SYMPTOMS
Few symptoms, so it is important to examine your cat regularly. The cat may lick at embedded ticks.

WHAT TO DO
- Treat the cat at home with tick spray, powder, collar or medicated bath made especially for use on cats. (Follow the accompanying directions carefully. If you give the cat a flea collar, **do not** also treat it with a flea bath. Using both can cause serious poisoning. Flea collars that are too tight or frequently moistened may cause irritation. Always restrain the cat before administering treatment. See **RESTRAINTS,** page 177.) Wait about half an hour, then remove the dead ticks with tweezers. Apply "tamed" iodine or other antiseptic to the bites.
- Apply tick powder or spray to the cat's bedding and the other areas it frequents. If the cat has ticks in cold weather, your home may be contaminated and a professional exterminator may be necessary.
- **Consult your veterinarian** if the cat does not respond to treatment.
- As a precaution, be sure to wash your hands thoroughly after you handle your cat. Ticks can be passed to other animals and humans, as can some of the diseases they carry.

PARASITES: INTERNAL

COCCIDIOSIS

SYMPTOMS
Diarrhea, with or without dark tar-like blood. Weight loss. The parasite is passed by contact with contaminated stool. Frequently affects kittens, to whom it can be fatal, particularly after contact with many other kittens and following periods of high stress.

WHAT TO DO
- **Consult your veterinarian.** Administer the follow-up treatment he prescribes. Responds well to treatment and usually does not recur.
- As a precaution, have the veterinarian analyze a specimen of your cat's stool once a year. Also have the analysis made before you buy a kitten or breed a female. If necessary, have the cat wormed. Coccidiosis is often overlooked by commercial breeders in routine wormings.

HOOKWORMS

SYMPTOMS
May include: Diarrhea, with or without dark or tar-like blood. (The parasite is not visible in the stool.) In advanced cases, the gums, tongue and inner linings of the eyelids become pale and whitish. Affects all ages but particularly dangerous to kittens. May be passed to a kitten before birth or through its mother's milk. Can also be contracted by contact with contaminated stool or surroundings.

WHAT TO DO

- Consult your veterinarian. Early treatment is important.
- Back home, administer the prescribed follow-up treatment and give the cat nourishing food to maintain its strength.

- To prevent reinfestation, maintain particularly good sanitation of all the areas the cat frequents.
- As a precaution, have the veterinarian analyze a specimen of your cat's stool once a year. Also have the analysis made before you buy a kitten or breed a female. If necessary, have the cat wormed.

ROUNDWORMS

SYMPTOMS

Stool or vomit may contain whitish, spaghetti-like coiled worms from 2 to 6 inches long. Other symptoms may include: "Potbelly." Dull coat. Listlessness. Restlessness. Diarrhea, in advanced cases. The parasite may be passed to a kitten before birth or through its mother's milk. Can also be contracted by contact with an affected cat or contaminated surroundings.

WHAT TO DO

- Consult your veterinarian. Early treatment is important.

- Back home, administer the prescribed follow-up treatment and give the cat nourishing food to maintain its strength. Be sure to wash your hands thoroughly whenever you handle the cat or clean its litter.
- To prevent reinfestation, change the cat's litter and disinfect its litter pan twice a week. Maintain particularly good sanitation of the litter area for one month. after starting treatment.
- As a precaution, have the veterinarian analyze a specimen of your cat's stool once a year. Also have the analysis made before you buy a kitten or breed a female. If necessary, have the cat wormed.

TAPEWORMS

SYMPTOMS

Flat, rice-like white or cream-colored segments 1/2 inch long may be seen around the cat's tail or in its droppings or bedding. (May be mistaken for MAGGOTS; see page 98.) The cat may scoot on its rear end. It may develop a ravenous appetite but does not gain weight or may actually lose it. The parasite can be passed to the cat when it eats infected fleas, prey or raw meat or fish. Routine stool analysis may fail to reveal the presence of tapeworm eggs.

WHAT TO DO

- Consult your veterinarian.
- Back home, administer the prescribed follow-up treatment and give the cat nourishing food to maintain its strength. Also treat the cat for **FLEAS**; see page 97. (Tapeworms are difficult to get rid of permanently because infected fleas can reinfest the cat and medications are not as potent as those used for other parasites.)
- As a precaution, do not let the cat eat prey or raw meat or fish.

TOXOPLASMOSIS

SYMPTOMS

Much of the time, there are no or hardly any symptoms. When symptoms are present, they may include: Depression. Loss of appetite. Pneumonia. In advanced cases, there may possibly be a wide range of other symptoms, depending on the part of the body that has been infected. (This protozoan parasite affects the intestines initially but then spreads to other areas of the body including the brain, liver, eyes and lungs. Toxoplasmosis should be suspected whenever an illness in any part of the body does not respond to the appropriate treatment.) The parasite can be passed to a kitten before birth by an affected mother. It can also be contracted by direct contact with contaminated cat feces or by eating infected raw meat, fish or prey.

WHAT TO DO

- Consult your veterinarian. Requires prolonged treatment.
- The parasite is highly contagious to almost every animal, including humans. It can cause permanent brain damage to unborn children. Pregnant women should not handle the litter pan of an infected cat.
- To protect the other members of your household, change the cat's litter and disinfect its litter pan daily. Wear gloves. Use ammonia or immerse the pan in boiling water. Wash your hands thoroughly when you are through.
- As a precaution, do not let your cat eat prey, raw meat or fish. Also try to keep it away from areas that may be contaminated by infected cat stool. The parasite eggs can live in soil for many months.

RESPIRATORY DISORDERS

ASTHMA-LIKE BRONCHIAL DISEASE

SYMPTOMS
Dry, hacking cough. Wheezing. In advanced cases, may progress to very severe breathing difficulties. An allergic respiratory disease in which the passages to the lungs become constricted. Caused by an allergic reaction to pollens, grasses, dust or other irritants. Usually develops at certain times of the year, particularly in the spring. Tends to be recurrent. Usually not very severe.

WHAT TO DO
- **Consult your veterinarian.**
- Coughing is never normal in a cat and should always be brought to your veterinarian's attention.

OBSTRUCTION OF THE NASAL PASSAGES

SYMPTOMS
Pawing at the nose. Sneezing. Nasal discharge or blood from one or both nostrils. The cat may shake or throw its head violently in an effort to dislodge the obstruction to its breathing.

WHAT TO DO
- **Consult your veterinarian.** Foreign objects can usually be removed. Tumors require difficult surgery.

PNEUMONIA

SYMPTOMS
Loss of appetite. Severe depression. Fever. Dehydration. Extreme weakness. Deep, moist cough, sometimes with gagging. In severe cases: Rapid, shallow, difficult breathing. The cat may carry its head elevated and show pain if lifted by the chest. The tongue, gums and inner linings of the eyelids become progressively more blue. Caused by an inflammation of the lungs resulting from an inhalation of swallowed or vomited material, or from bacteria, fungi or a viral infection.

WHAT TO DO
- **Consult your veterinarian. Early treatment is important.**
- Your cat will require good nursing care at home. Keep it comfortable and quiet and avoid putting it in stressful situations that may cause it to breathe heavily.
- Coughing is never normal in a cat and should always be brought to the veterinarian's attention.

PNEUMOTHORAX

SYMPTOMS
Severe labored breathing. The gums, tongue and inner linings of the eyelids may become progressively more blue. The cat's abdomen may rise and fall as it tries to breathe. Caused by air entering the chest from a ruptured lung or a puncture or laceration in the chest. The air surrounds and presses against the lungs, preventing them from expanding fully as the cat tries to breathe.

WHAT TO DO
- **Consult your veterinarian. Early treatment is important.**
- After treatment, watch the cat closely for recurring symptoms that indicate air is still leaking into its chest.

PULMONARY EDEMA

SYMPTOMS
Coughing. Difficulty breathing. Shallow, rapid breathing through the mouth. Wheezing. Severe anxiety. The cat may refuse to lie down. Caused by an abnormal accumulation of fluid in the lungs. Usually a complication of other conditions such as congestive heart failure, heart muscle disease and brain tumor. Depending on the cause, may develop suddenly or slowly. May occur suddenly as a result of an allergic reaction, electric shock, drowning, or a snake or spider bite.

WHAT TO DO
- **Consult your veterinarian. Early treatment is very important.**
- Carefully transport the cat to the vet, making sure it has plenty of cool, fresh air. See **TRANSPORTING A CAT,** page 172.
- Additional stress will worsen the symptoms, so try to keep the cat from becoming excited, particularly while you are taking it to the vet.

PYOTHORAX

SYMPTOMS

Progressive difficulty breathing. Loss of appetite. Depression. High temperature. A very serious bacterial infection in which pus collects around the lungs, preventing them from functioning properly. Usually caused by an untreated bite wound in or around the chest which abscesses to the inside of the chest.

WHAT TO DO

• **Consult your veterinarian.**

• Can be prevented by having your veterinarian promptly treat all bite wounds and abscesses around the chest and neck.

REVERSE SNEEZE SYNDROME

SYMPTOMS

Recurrent episodes of what sounds like sneezing, snoring or snorting, except that the cat is drawing air in rather than expelling it out. May last between 15 seconds and 1 minute. The cat may also show some **respiratory difficulty.** Can be caused by a throat spasm or postnasal drip.

WHAT TO DO

• **Consult your veterinarian** if the condition occurs frequently or lasts for extended periods.

SKELETAL DISORDERS

NUTRITIONAL SECONDARY HYPERPARATHYROIDISM

SYMPTOMS

Painful, swollen elbows and front wrist joints. The toes are widespread and splayed outward. Fractures, with little or no reason. A major disease of kittens in which calcium is drawn from the bones, causing them to become progressively thin and fragile and subject to fractures. Caused by an imbalance of calcium and phosphorus in the diet. A common result of an all meat diet, especially if it consists of heart, liver and kidneys.

WHAT TO DO

• **Consult your veterinarian.** He may prescribe calcium supplements or recommend a diet that contains a proper balance of calcium and phosphorus.
• As a prevention, avoid feeding your kitten an all meat diet, particularly one made up of heart, liver and kidneys.

OSTEOARTHRITIS (DEGENERATIVE JOINT DISEASE)

SYMPTOMS

Tenderness and pain. Limping. Enlargement of the joint. A rubbing or grating sound may be heard when the joint is moved. A common chronic disease of the moveable joints involving deterioration of the cartilage. To protect itself, the joint makes structural changes such as growing excess bone. Can be the result of injury, a poor fit in the joint or misuse of the joint. May affect more than one joint. The condition often worsens as the cat grows older.

WHAT TO DO

• **Consult your veterinarian.** Treatment is aimed at relieving pain, restoring the function of the joint and preventing further degeneration. Ongoing medication may be required.

• To reduce stress on the joint, keep the cat's weight as low as possible and avoid vigorous or extended exercise.

OSTEOMYELITIS

SYMPTOMS

The cat has a bone wound that does not heal. The wound drains fluid and pus and may develop a foul odor. The **area around the wound is hot, swollen and painful.** A bacterial infection within a bone commonly caused by bite wounds, compound fractures, bone surgery or other conditions where bacteria can reach the bone and the blood circulation in the area has been disturbed. Occasionally caused by a fungus. Usually affects the long bones. As the infection progresses, it begins to eat away the calcium and weaken the bone.

WHAT TO DO
• **Consult your veterinarian.** Surgery is usually required to clean out all infected material. Long-term hospital and home treatment will probably be necessary.

TRAUMA

SYMPTOMS
Less severe cases may include: Sprains, strains and bruises. Soreness. Reduced use of the affected part. Limping. More severe cases may include: Fractures or dislocations, most commonly in the leg or thigh. Acute, severe pain. Swelling. The cat carries its leg lame. Severe fractures may make a grating sound when the affected parts are moved. A sudden injury to the bones caused by car accidents, falls or severe blows.

WHAT TO DO
• **Consult your veterinarian.**
• **For emergency treatment of a severe trauma:** See **BREAKS: FRACTURES & DISLOCATIONS,** page 129.
• As a precaution, always consult your veterinarian in cases of prolonged mild or intermittent lameness.

SKIN DISORDERS

ABSCESS

SYMPTOMS
Soft swelling on the limbs or elsewhere on the body. The affected areas are tender and painful, and the cat objects to being touched there but does not otherwise appear to be ill. In advanced stages, the swollen areas become open draining sores. A localized, encapsulated pus-forming infection under the skin. A common result of animal bites, fights and untreated injuries. Most likely to occur in older unneutered males.

WHAT TO DO
• **Consult your veterinarian.**
• **For home care:** Apply hot compresses to help relieve discomfort and bring the abscess to a head. When the abscess opens, keep the area clean of discharge and debris.
• To prevent abscesses, treat all skin wounds promptly.

ACNE

SYMPTOMS

Pustules, blackheads or small cysts on the underside of the chin and where the chin meets the lips. These areas are affected because the cat cannot reach them effectively to keep them clean. Often a recurrent problem.

WHAT TO DO
• **Consult your veterinarian.**

ANAPHYLAXIS

SYMPTOMS
Tremendous sudden swelling and thickening of the skin on the face, lips and eyelids. The eyes may be swollen nearly closed and the mouth greatly distorted. The cat's head may seem too large for its body. The cat may scratch violently at itself. The female's vulva may become swollen. An allergic reaction of the skin caused by something that has been eaten, inhaled, injected or touched. Sometimes develops without any notable change in diet or environment. Not usually recurrent.

WHAT TO DO
• **Consult your veterinarian.** In mild cases, the cat usually recovers without treatment.
• **For home care:** Administer a child's dosage of antihistamine syrup or antihistamine tablet. See **ADMINISTERING LIQUID MEDICINE,** page 188, or **ADMINISTERING PILLS,** page 189.
• As a precaution, always advise your veterinarian of any allergic reaction.

BACTERIAL SKIN INFECTION (PYODERMA)

Surface infections develop small pustules, which may rupture. The cat may lick or scratch at the irritated area. The affected skin becomes reddened and angry. As the infection progresses and affects deeper layers of skin, it may ulcerate, ooze pus and spread to cover larger areas of the body. Caused by the bacteria normally on the skin becoming infective. Often results from untreated cases of flea allergy dermatitis. May also be a result of skin irritation due to injury, moisture or collected debris. Often seen in connection with malnutrition or parasite infestation where the cat has become run-down. Tends to be recurrent, particularly when the deeper layers of skin are affected.

- **Consult your veterinarian. Early treatment is important**. May require lengthy treatment. Must be completely cured to prevent the progress of the infection or later recurrence.
- Try to prevent an affected cat from biting or licking the infected areas.

FLEA ALLERGY DERMATITIS

Hair loss and extremely reddened skin, usually around the back and the base of the tail. Severe scratching and chewing at the irritated areas. Possible scabs or infection. Dark specks of flea excrement on the cat's skin that turn red when moistened with water. Fleas may or may not be seen. An allergic reaction to the saliva of fleas. Occurs whenever fleas are prevalent. Affects some cats but not others.

- **Consult your veterinarian** for treatment of the skin condition.
- Treat the affected cat and all other cats and dogs in your household for **FLEAS**; see page 97.
- Observe for **BACTERIAL SKIN INFECTION**; see above.

HEAD MANGE

Hair loss and scaly, reddened skin, especially on the face, edges of the ears and forelegs. Scabs. Pustules. Severe continuous scratching.

- **Consult your veterinarian. Early treatment is important.** Head mange reproduces very quickly.
- Treat the cat's bedding and the other areas it frequents with flea or tick insecticide made especially for use on cats.
- Head mange is highly contagious to other pets and humans. As a precaution, treat the unaffected animals in your home once a week until the affected cat is cured. (Treat a dog with medication made especially for use on dogs.)

HIVES

Small areas of localized swelling that may be limited to one region or distributed all over the cat. The cat may have a "checkerboard" or spotted appearance from the hair in the affected areas pointing in a slightly different direction from the surrounding hair. Temporary thickening of the affected skin. An allergic reaction of the skin caused by something that has been eaten, inhaled, injected or touched. Sometimes develops without any notable change in diet or environment. Not usually recurrent.

- **Consult your veterinarian.** In mild cases, the cat usually recovers without treatment.
- **For home care:** Administer a child's dosage of antihistamine syrup or antihistamine tablet. See **ADMINISTERING LIQUID MEDICINE,** page 188, or **ADMINISTERING PILLS,** page 189.
- As a precaution, always advise your veterinarian of any allergic reaction.

LICK GRANULOMA

Constant licking or biting at one spot, usually on top of the front paw near the wrist. Loss of hair around the bitten area. The affected skin becomes fat and angry looking. As the condition progresses, the skin thickens and may ulcerate, become infected and ooze pus. The

cause is unknown but may begin with a scrape, insect bite or other irritation.

- **Consult your veterinarian. Early treatment is necessary to prevent serious infection.** An important part of the treatment involves preventing the cat from licking at itself while the area heals. Bandages or an Elizabethan collar are usually used to prevent this further irritation. When prevented from licking the affected spot, the cat may begin to lick a new spot above the bandage or on the opposite paw.
- Continue to watch the cat after treatment has been completed. The condition tends to recur.

RINGWORM

SYMPTOMS

May include: Well-defined round or oval scaly patches, often with stubbly hair, on the head or elsewhere on the body. A skin infection caused by any of the many types of fungi. Usually results from contact with an infected animal (most often a cat) or contaminated hair.

WHAT TO DO

- **Consult your veterinarian. Early treatment is important** and should be continued until all symptoms are completely eliminated. May take a considerable time.
- Some forms of ringworm are highly contagious to cats, dogs and humans, so it may be necessary to isolate the affected cat. As a further precaution, keep the cat's area free of loose hair.

RODENT ULCER

SYMPTOMS

An unsightly thick, protruding ulcer near the center of the upper lip or elsewhere around the mouth. May spread to other parts of the body the cat licks at. A chronic condition of unknown cause. Can become cancerous.

WHAT TO DO

- **Consult your veterinarian. Can disfigure the cat's face if not treated promptly.** Generally improves with care but is recurrent. Surgery is usually required if the ulcer has become cancerous; see **SQUAMOUS CELL CARCINOMA,** page 83.

SEBORRHEA

SYMPTOMS

There are 3 different types of seborrhea: dry, oily and dermatitis. SYMPTOMS OF DRY SEBORRHEA: White, gray or silver scabs scattered throughout the cat's hair in little crusts. SYMPTOMS OF OILY SEBORRHEA: Greasy, scaly patches. Foul, rancid odor. SYMPTOMS OF DERMATITIS SEBORRHEA: Scaly or oily patches all over the cat's body. Scratching. Reddened skin. A chronic skin condition caused by an increased production of skin oils and scales. The cause is unknown.

WHAT TO DO

- **Consult your veterinarian.** Long-term treatment may be necessary. Seborrhea can be controlled, but not completely cured. Some cases respond to hormone therapy.
- If your cat has oily seborrhea, shampoo it frequently to control the objectionable odor.

WARTS

SYMPTOMS

Small hard gray or white, rough-surfaced masses on the skin or inside the mouth. The cat may lick or chew at them. May bleed if irritated. May occur individually or in groups. Caused by a virus. Most common in older cats.

WHAT TO DO

- **Consult your veterinarian.** May have to be removed surgically.
- Continue to observe an affected cat after treatment has been completed. Warts can recur, ever after surgical removal.

TRAUMA

HEAD INJURY

SYMPTOMS

Unconsciousness or semiconsciousness. Bleeding from the face, nose, mouth or ears. Fractures of the bones in the face. Convulsions may occur if the injury creates pressure on the brain. Caused by a sudden injury to the head. Commonly the result of a car accident, fall or severe blow. Potentially serious because it may affect the brain or the delicate structures of the eyes, ears, nose or mouth.

WHAT TO DO

• **Consult your veterinarian.**

LAMENESS

SYMPTOMS

Vary with severity. In a fairly mild case involving muscle or soft tissue injury, the cat may limp with pain or discomfort but still puts its weight on its leg when it walks. If there is a more severe injury such as a cracked bone, fracture, dislocation or serious muscle damage, the cat will not use the leg as it walks but carry it up close to its body away from the ground.

WHAT TO DO

• **Consult your veterinarian** if the cat carries its leg.

RUPTURED BLADDER

SYMPTOMS

Repeated futile attempts to urinate. After several hours or more, additional symptoms may include: Painfully distended belly. Vomiting. Loss of appetite. Depression. Dehydration. A sudden breaking of the bladder caused by being hit by a car or some other severe blow to the belly while the bladder is full.

WHAT TO DO

• **Consult your veterinarian. Early treatment is important.** Surgical repair is required.
• A ruptured bladder is to be suspected whenever a cat has had a serious accident involving a sharp blow to the belly. As a precaution, observe the cat closely for up to 48 hours to make sure it is still producing urine.

URINARY DISORDERS

BACTERIAL CYSTITIS

SYMPTOMS

Frequent efforts to urinate, producing only small amounts of urine. Straining. Pain. The cat stays in the urinating position longer than normal. It wets in unusual places such as the sink or bathtub. Blood in the urine. A bacterial infection of the bladder. Usually travels up the urinary tract from the outside as a result of an injury or some other cause. More common in males than females. Cats that do not get the chance to void their bladders frequently are predisposed to this condition, as well as to urolithiasis.

WHAT TO DO

• **Consult your veterinarian. May become a chronic condition and lead to more serious urinary problems if left untreated.**
• After treatment, watch the cat carefully for symptoms of recurrence.

END STAGE KIDNEY DISEASE

SYMPTOMS

Cats whose kidneys function only marginally are usually excessively thirsty and urinate frequently. The gums, tongue and inner linings of their eyelids may also become progressively more pale. As a result of stress or further loss of kidney function, additional symptoms may include: **Vomiting. Diarrhea. Loss of appetite. Depression. Weakness. Dehydration.** The result of damage to the kidneys from any number of other kidney diseases. May develop slowly as kidney function is lost because of aging or chronic or repeated kidney illness, or more quickly as a result of serious kidney damage. Symptoms usually appear when the cat is placed under stress from such things as fighting, being in the hot sun, going to a veterinarian or cattery, or undergoing any sort of illness.

WHAT TO DO
- **Consult your veterinarian.** Treatment is aimed at reducing stress and maintaining the cat's balance with its environment so that the remaining minimal kidney function suffices to serve its needs. The vet may prescribe a special diet containing a small amount of high quality protein.

PYOMETRA (UTERINE INFECTION)

SYMPTOMS

Excessive thirst and urination. The cat has difficulty holding its urine and wets in the house. May also include foul-smelling vulvar discharge containing blood or pus. In severe cases, there may also be vomiting and dehydration. A bacterial infection of the uterus caused by an underlying hormonal imbalance. Occurs only in female cats, usually within a month after being in heat. Most common in females over 5 years old.

WHAT TO DO
- **Consult your veterinarian. Early treatment is essential.** Surgery is usually required. An affected animal may also develop other hormone-related conditions such as **MAMMARY TUMORS,** page 83.
- Can be prevented by spaying the cat when it is young.

UROLITHIASIS (URINARY CALCULI)

SYMPTOMS

IF THERE IS A PARTIAL URINARY OBSTRUCTION: Frequent efforts to urinate, producing only small amounts of urine. Straining. Pain. The cat stays in the urinating position longer than normal. It wets in unusual places such as the sink or bathtub. The urine contains blood or sand-like material. IF THE URINARY OBSTRUCTION IS TOTAL: No urinating. Intense pain. Tender abdomen. Acute distress. A chronic condition caused by sand-like material accumulating in the bladder and obstructing the passage of urine out of the body. Most common in males because of their narrow urinary opening, but also affects females.

WHAT TO DO
- **Consult your veterinarian. Prompt treatment is essential. Total obstruction can be fatal.**
- An affected cat should be watched closely for reduced production of urine.
- To help prevent recurrence: Add salt to the cat's diet to encourage drinking and make sure that plenty of water is available.
- If the condition recurs in a male, surgery may be necessary to widen its urinary opening.

ALPHABETICAL INDEX OF ILLNESSES AND DISORDERS

EMERGENCIES: FIRST-AID PROCEDURES

First aid is not a substitute for professional veterinary care. If your cat becomes seriously injured or ill, you should always try to get the immediate assistance of a veterinarian. Unfortunately, this isn't always possible. Emergencies have a way of happening when help isn't available right away, and if they aren't dealt with promptly, the cat's life may be jeopardized. Under such circumstances, your ability to provide quick, effective first aid may make the difference between your cat's life and death.

This section provides the most up-to-date first-aid procedures for all the common emergencies that are most likely to afflict your pet. To help you act quickly and correctly, each procedure combines clear, simple instructions printed in large type with easy to follow step-by-step illustrations. As a further help, the back cover of this book is thumb indexed to give you immediate access to the relevant procedures. Each procedure is also listed in the **CONTENTS** in the front of the book, and the symptoms for all emergencies are included in the **SYMPTOM RECOGNITION INDEX** that begins on page 65.

There are several crucial points to keep in mind whenever you have to come to your cat's aid:

• It is, of course, terribly distressing to see a cherished pet suffering from an illness or injury, but if you are to alleviate the emergency you must do your best to remain calm and clearheaded so you can follow the appropriate procedures correctly.

• If you are unsure about the nature or extent of an emergency, see **ASSESSING THE EMERGENCY,** page 111, before attempting any first aid. There are times when doing the incorrect thing can be more injurious than not doing anything at all. The **SYMPTOM RECOGNITION INDEX** will also help you determine what is wrong.

• An injured cat that is still conscious should always be restrained before it is examined or treated. Restraint places the animal under your control, prevents it from injuring you or worsening its own condition and makes it easier for you to administer first aid. Pain, fright and confusion can cause a normally gentle pet to become vicious and strike out at a helping hand offered too quickly. We suggest that you study the section on **RESTRAINTS,** page 177, to acquaint yourself with this single most important aspect of emergency care.

ASSESSING THE EMERGENCY

IMPORTANT

- Always approach an injured cat with caution. Speak in a gentle, reassuring voice. If possible, protect your hands with gloves.

- **Consult your veterinarian as soon as possible for any injury that seems serious.** See **TRANSPORTING AN INJURED CAT,** pages 172-173.

1 Restrain the cat if it is conscious. See **RE-STRAINTS, pages 177-185.**

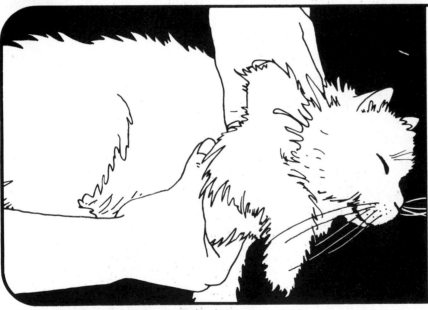

2 Check the heartbeat by gently squeezing the lower third of the cat's chest between your thumb and fingers. If no heartbeat is felt, see **HEART FAILURE,** pages 157-158.

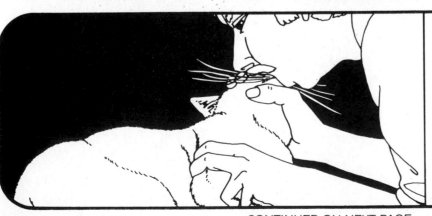

3 Check the cat's breathing. If necessary, see **BREATHING: ARTIFICIAL RESPIRATION,** pages 131-133.

CONTINUED ON NEXT PAGE

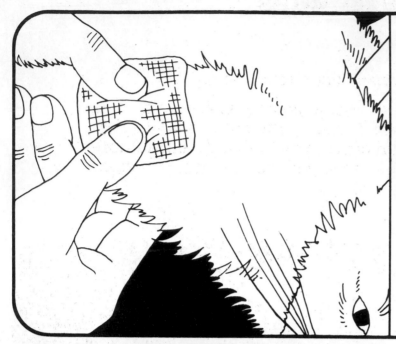

4 **Check for bleeding.** Quickly and gently examine the cat's head and body for injuries. Make sure not to overlook any concealed wounds. Control the most serious bleeding first. See **BLEEDING: CUTS & WOUNDS,** pages 121-127.

5 If there are burns or stains on the cat's mouth or other signs of poisoning (pills, chemicals, etc.), see **POISONING,** pages 164-169.

6 If the cat is unconscious or unresponsive, treat for **SHOCK,** pages 170-171.

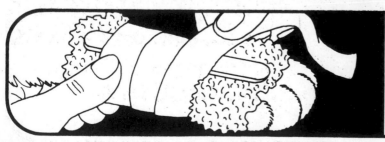

7 For broken bones, see **BREAKS: FRACTURES & DISLOCATIONS,** page 129.

BITES & STINGS

ANIMAL BITES

IMPORTANT

- **If the skin is penetrated, consult your veterinarian.**

- Try to capture or confine the other animal for examination. Take care not to be bitten yourself. If you kill the other animal, keep its head intact. The head can provide the public health authorities with information that may save your cat a long quarantine.

- Observe for **SHOCK,** pages 170-171.

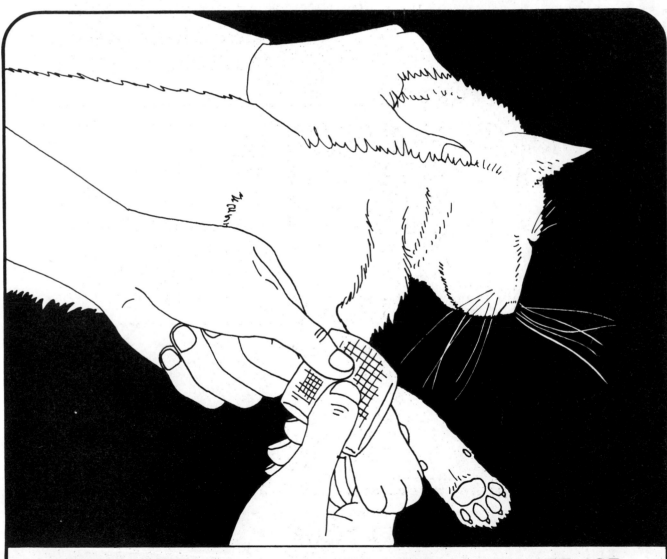

1 Restrain the cat. See **RESTRAINTS, pages 177-185.** Control the bleeding. See **BLEEDING: CUTS & WOUNDS,** pages 121-124.

CONTINUED ON NEXT PAGE

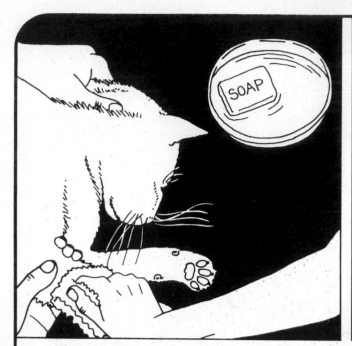

2 Wash the wound with soap and water. Apply "tamed" iodine or other antiseptic. **Do not** use ointments or other medications.

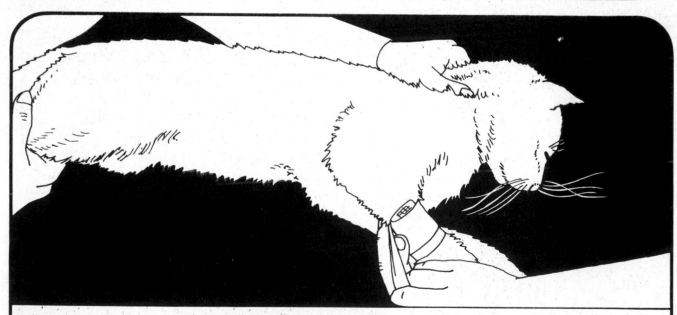

3 Apply a sterile dressing or clean cloth, and hold it firmly in place with a bandage. **Do not** bind too tightly.

BITES & STINGS

INSECTS

IMPORTANT

- **Consult your veterinarian as soon as possible** for bites and stings from **Black Widow** and **Brown Recluse Spiders, Scorpions** and **Tarantulas,** particularly if the cat is subject to an allergic reaction or is bitten on the mouth or eye.

- Observe for **SHOCK,** pages 170-171.

BEE (WASP, HORNET & YELLOW JACKET)

NOTE: Consult your veterinarian as soon as possible if the cat is subject to an allergic reaction or if there is severe swelling anywhere on its body. Also observe for **SHOCK,** pages 170-171, and watch breathing closely. If necessary, see **BREATHING: ARTIFICIAL RESPIRATION,** pages 131-133.

SYMPTOMS: Pain. Local swelling. Itching. Allergic reaction will also cause shock, unconsciousness and severe swelling.

FIRST AID: Restrain the cat. See RESTRAINTS, pages 177-185. For a bee sting, remove the venom sac by scraping gently, not squeezing. (Wasps, hornets and yellow jackets do not leave venom sacs.) Wash the wound with soap and water. Administer 1/2 teaspoon antihistamine syrup or 1/2 antihistamine tablet. See **ADMINISTERING LIQUID MEDICINE,** page 188, or **ADMINISTERING PILLS,** pages 189-190. For severe reactions, follow first aid for **BLACK WIDOW SPIDER.**

BLACK WIDOW SPIDER

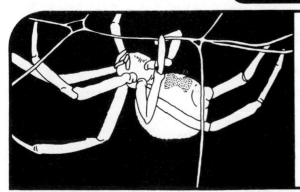

SYMPTOMS: Severe pain. Difficulty breathing. Swelling.

FIRST AID: Restrain the cat. See RESTRAINTS, pages 177-185. Watch breathing closely. If it stops, see **BREATHING: ARTIFICIAL RESPIRATION,** pages 131-133. Keep the cat

CONTINUED ON NEXT PAGE

BLACK WIDOW SPIDER, CONTINUED

quiet and avoid unnecessary movement. Keep the affected part below heart level. Place a constricting band about 1 inch wide 2 to 4 inches above the wound. **Do not** bind too tightly. You should be able to slide your finger under it. Apply ice wrapped in a cloth. Remove the band after 30 minutes. Administer 1/2 teaspoon antihistamine syrup or 1/2 antihistamine tablet. See **ADMINISTERING LIQUID MEDICINE,** page 188, or **ADMINISTERING PILLS,** pages 189-190.

BROWN RECLUSE SPIDER

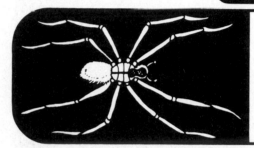

SYMPTOMS: The bite may be hardly noticed, but hours later severe pain, swelling and blisters occur.

FIRST AID: Follow first aid for **BLACK WIDOW SPIDER.**

SCORPION

SYMPTOMS: Excruciating pain at the sting. Swelling. Fever. Convulsions. Coma.

FIRST AID: Restrain the cat. See RE-STRAINTS, pages 177-185. Wash the wound with soap and water. Cover lightly with a sterile dressing or clean cloth. For severe reactions, follow first aid for **BLACK WIDOW SPIDER.**

TARANTULA

SYMPTOMS: May vary from pin prick to severe wound.

FIRST AID: Restrain the cat. See RE-STRAINTS, pages 177-185. Wash the wound with soap and water. Cover lightly with a sterile dressing or clean cloth. For severe reactions, follow first aid for **BLACK WIDOW SPIDER.**

BITES & STINGS

PORCUPINE QUILLS

- Carefully check the cat's paws, face and mouth for quills. If there are many quills or quills in the eyes or mouth, have your veterinarian remove them.

- Over the next week continue to check for quills and abscesses or infections. Broken quills often take that long to rise to the surface.

1 **Restrain the cat. See RESTRAINTS, pages 177-185.** Position the cat so the quills are exposed. Place one finger on each side and close to the quill.

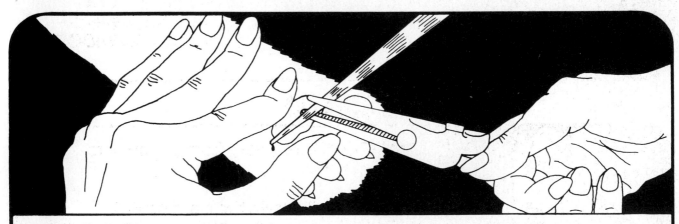

2 Grasp the quill near the skin with a needlenose pliers or your thumb and index finger. Avoid grasping the cat's fur.

CONTINUED ON NEXT PAGE

PORCUPINE QUILLS
CONTINUED

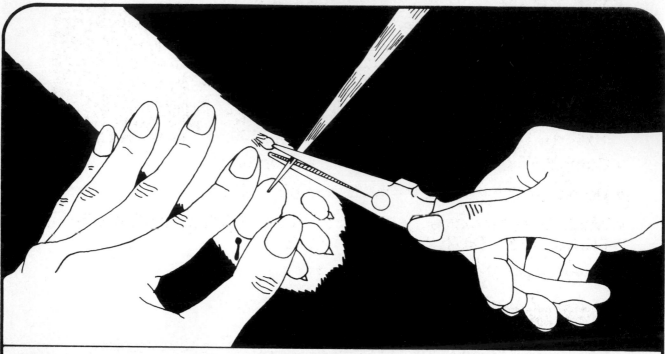

3 Using a quick, jerking motion, pull the quill straight out. **Do not** pull at an angle.

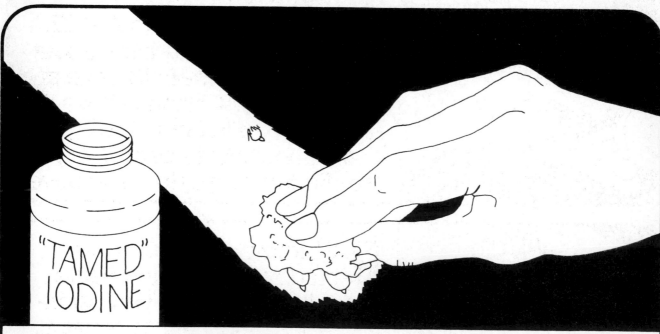

"TAMED" IODINE

4 Treat the wound with "tamed" iodine or other antiseptic.

BITES & STINGS

SNAKEBITE

IMPORTANT

- To determine if the bite is from a poisonous snake, look for fang marks at the wound. **If nonpoisonous, follow Step 4 only.**

POISONOUS

NONPOISONOUS

- **Consult your veterinarian as soon as possible.**

- **Do not** let the cat walk or move the affected part.

- Watch breathing closely. If necessary, see **BREATHING: ARTIFICIAL RESPIRATION,** pages 131-133.

- Observe for **SHOCK,** pages 170-171.

SYMPTOMS

Pain. Swelling. May also include vomiting, difficulty breathing, weakness, paralysis, convulsions.

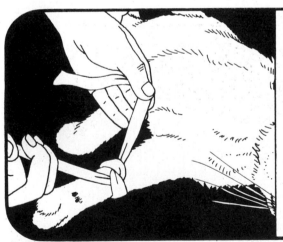

1 **Restrain the cat. See RESTRAINTS, pages 177-185.** Apply a constricting band about 1 inch wide between the bite and the heart 2 to 4 inches above the puncture. **Do not** bind too tightly. The wound should ooze. Keep the affected part below heart level.

2 Sterilize a knife or razor blade over an open flame, and make a **shallow vertical incision 1/2 inch long over each fang mark. Do not** cut deeply or crisscross.

CONTINUED ON NEXT PAGE

119

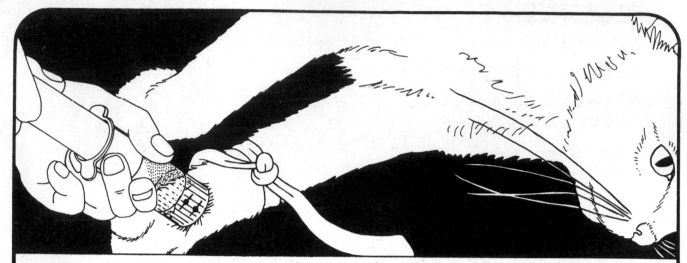

3 Draw the venom from the wound with a suction cup or your mouth, if it is free of open sores. Maintain suction for 30 minutes. If swelling reaches the band, leave it in place and apply a second band 2 to 4 inches above the first.

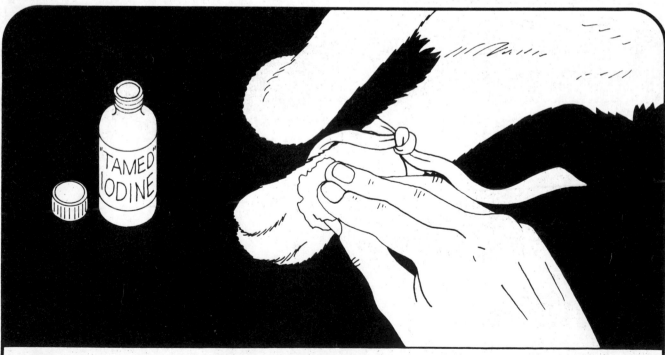

"TAMED" IODINE

4 Wash thoroughly with soap and water and apply "tamed" iodine or other antiseptic.

BLEEDING: CUTS & WOUNDS

DIRECT PRESSURE

IMPORTANT

- Consult your veterinarian for any serious bleeding.

- Observe for **SHOCK,** pages 170-171.

- First try to control the bleeding by **DIRECT PRESSURE;** see below.

- If serious blood loss continues and becomes critical, apply a **TOURNIQUET** as a last resort; see pages 122-124.

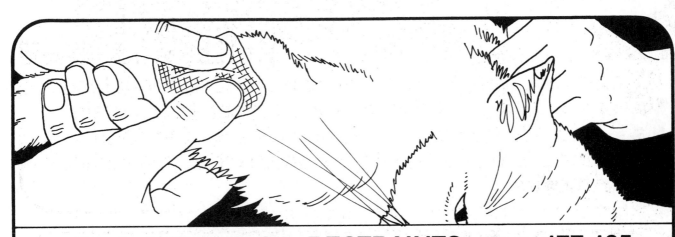

1 **Restrain the cat. See RESTRAINTS, pages 177-185.** Press a heavy gauze compress or clean cloth directly over the wound to control the bleeding.

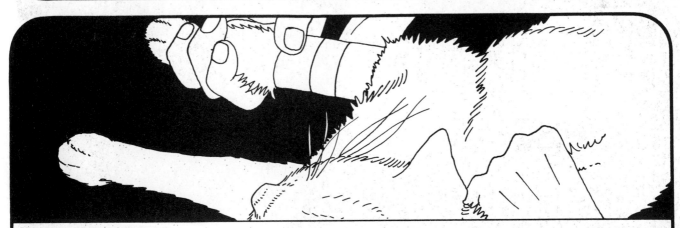

2 Maintain direct pressure by bandaging the compress firmly in place with adhesive tape. If bleeding does not stop, increase pressure by taping more tightly.

TOURNIQUET

IMPORTANT

- Consult your veterinarian as soon as possible.

- **Do not use except in a critical emergency where it is a matter of life over limb.** Always try **DIRECT PRESSURE** first; see page 121.

- The tourniquet band should be about 1 inch wide.

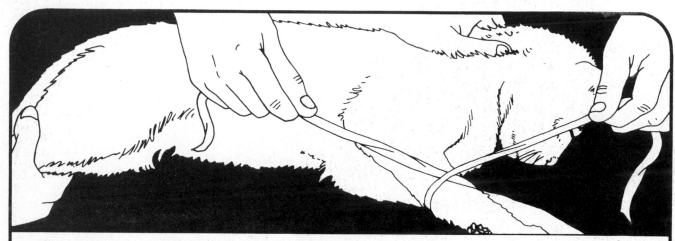

1 **Restrain the cat. See RESTRAINTS, pages 177-185.** Place the tourniquet band over the artery to be compressed, **slightly above** the wound. If a joint intervenes, position the band above the joint.

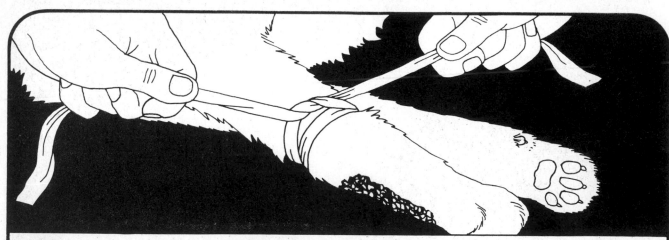

2 Wrap the band tightly around the limb twice, and tie a half knot.

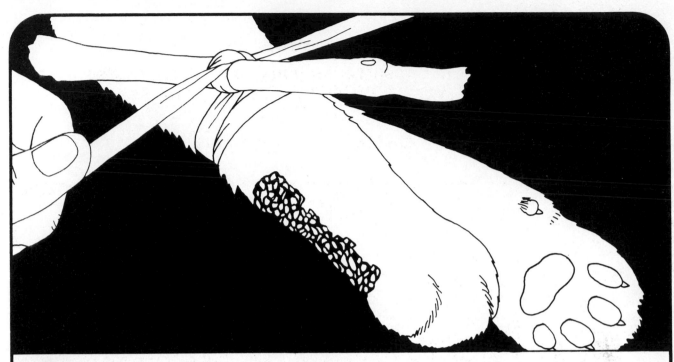

3 Place a short, strong stick on the band, and complete the knot on the top of the stick.

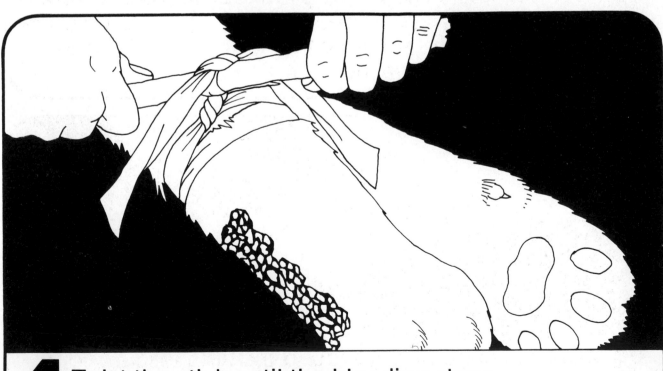

4 Twist the stick until the bleeding stops.

CONTINUED ON NEXT PAGE

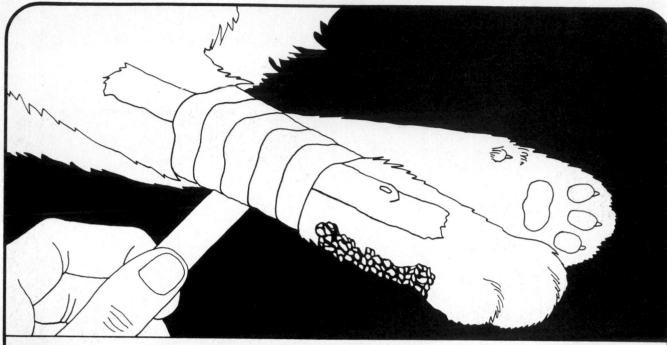

5 Secure the stick in place with adhesive tape. **Do not** loosen unless a veterinarian so advises.

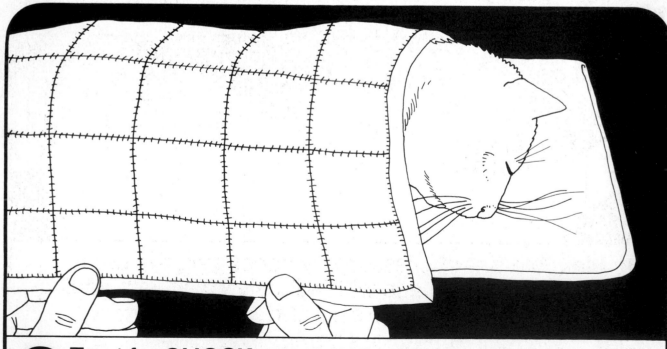

6 Treat for **SHOCK,** pages 170-171, and **get to a veterinarian immediately.**

BLEEDING: CUTS & WOUNDS

AMPUTATIONS

IMPORTANT

- **Stay calm and act quickly. Bleeding must be stopped.**
- **Consult your veterinarian as soon as possible.**

1 **Restrain the cat. See RESTRAINTS, pages 177-185.** Control the bleeding by pressing a heavy gauze compress or clean cloth directly over the wound.

2 Maintain direct pressure by bandaging the compress firmly in place with adhesive tape. If bleeding does not stop, increase pressure by taping more tightly. If serious blood loss continues and becomes critical, a **TOURNIQUET** may be necessary as a last resort; see pages 122-124.

BLEEDING: CUTS & WOUNDS

IMPALED OBJECTS

IMPORTANT

- **Get to a veterinarian as soon as possible.**

- **Do not** move the cat off an impaling object unless its life is in imminent danger. If you must, remove it as gently as possible, tend to the wounds immediately and treat for shock. See **BLEEDING: DIRECT PRESSURE**, page 121, and **SHOCK**, pages 170-171.

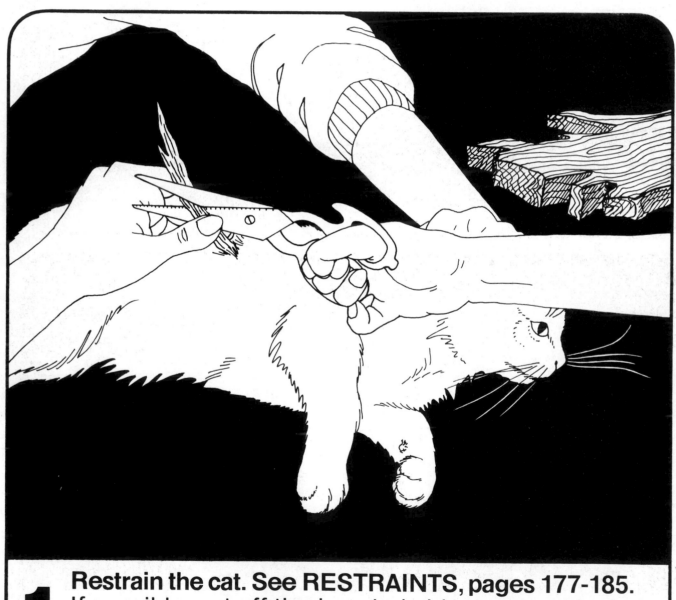

1 **Restrain the cat. See RESTRAINTS, pages 177-185.** If possible, cut off the impaled object several inches from the wound without moving or removing it.

BLEEDING: CUTS & WOUNDS

IMPALED OBJECTS

2 Place bulky dressings around the object.

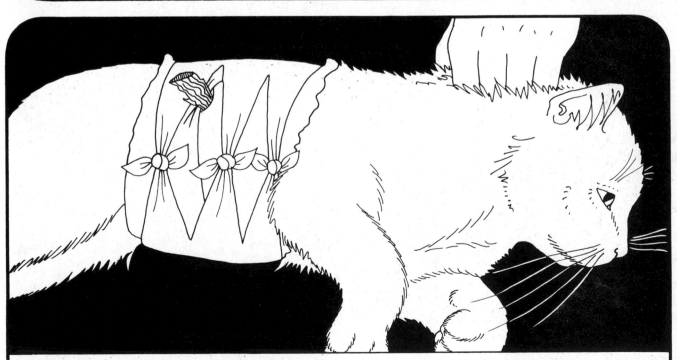

3 Secure the dressings in place with bandages. Observe for **SHOCK,** pages 170-171.

BLEEDING: CUTS & WOUNDS

INTERNAL BLEEDING

IMPORTANT

- To be suspected if the cat has had a sharp blow or crushing injury to the body.

- **Do not** give the cat anything to drink.

- **Consult your veterinarian.**

- Observe for **SHOCK,** pages 170-171.

SYMPTOMS

There is usually no visible bleeding, although the cat may bleed from its ears, nose, mouth or anus. Progressive weakness. Pale or blue gums. Progressive difficulty breathing. May also include bloody vomit, excrement or urine.

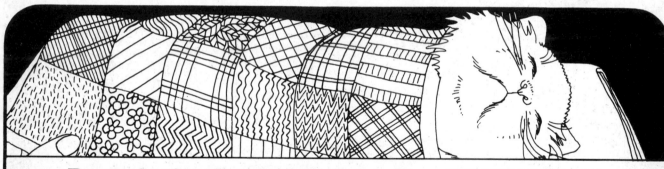

1 **Restrain the cat if necessary. See RESTRAINTS, pages 177-185.** Keep the cat lying down and covered lightly.

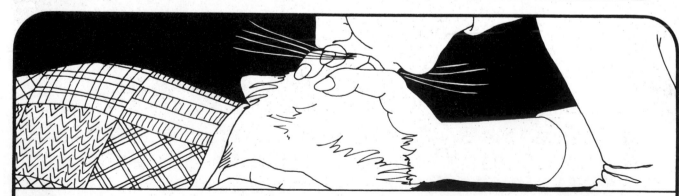

2 Watch breathing closely. If necessary, see **BREATH-ING: ARTIFICIAL RESPIRATION,** pages 131-133.

BREAKS: FRACTURES & DISLOCATIONS

LOWER LEG, PAW, TOES & TAIL

IMPORTANT

- **Consult your veterinarian.**
- **Do not** treat fractures or dislocations other than of the lower leg, paw, toes or tail. **See your veterinarian immediately.**
- **Do not** try to reset dislocations yourself. Treat the same as fractures.
- Observe for **SHOCK,** pages 170-171.

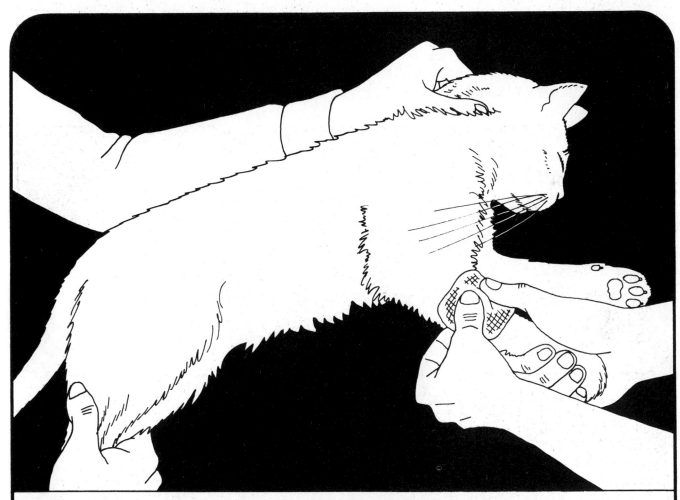

1 **Restrain the cat. See RESTRAINTS, pages 177-185.** If any bones protrude, control the bleeding with **DIRECT PRESSURE,** page 121, and cover the wound with a large clean dressing or cloth. **Do not** clean the wound.

CONTINUED ON NEXT PAGE

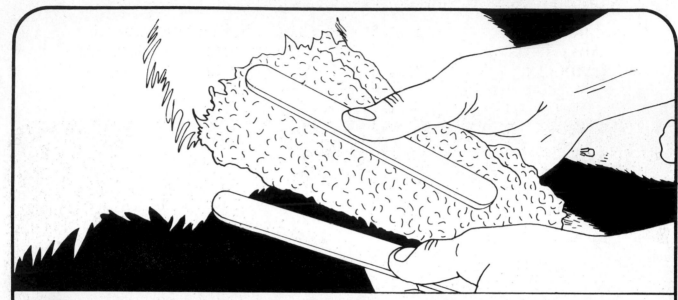

2 Wrap cotton batting or cloth around the entire bone for padding, then place tongue depressors or other splints on opposite sides of the break for rigidity. The splints should extend past the joints at both ends of the break.

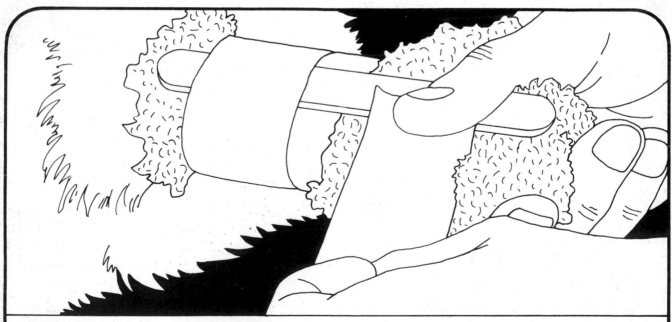

3 Wrap the splints in place with adhesive tape. **Do not** bind too tightly.

BREATHING: ARTIFICIAL RESPIRATION

IMPORTANT

- **Consult your veterinarian as soon as possible.**

- If the cat has drowned or inhaled vomit, liquid medication or other fluids, quickly suspend it by the rear feet for 15 seconds, giving 3 or 4 downward shakes to help drain the air passages.

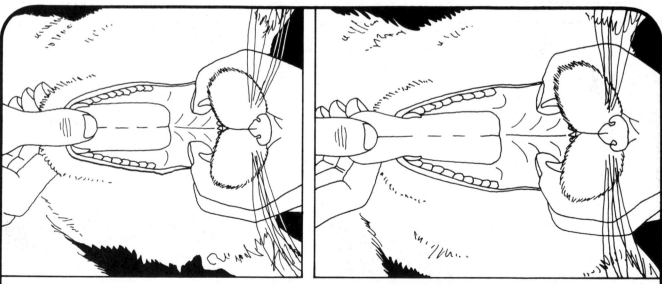

1 Place the cat on its side with its head extended. Remove its collar or harness.

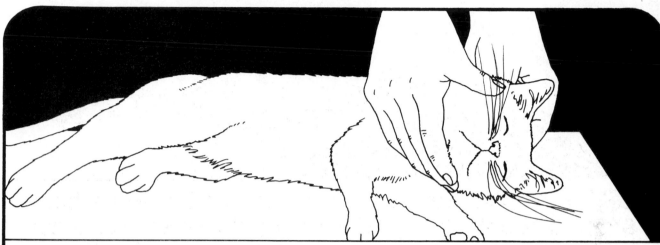

2 Open its mouth and cautiously pull out its tongue with your fingers or a cloth. Hold the tongue to keep the airway open. If necessary, clear out its mouth with your fingers or a cloth.

CONTINUED ON NEXT PAGE

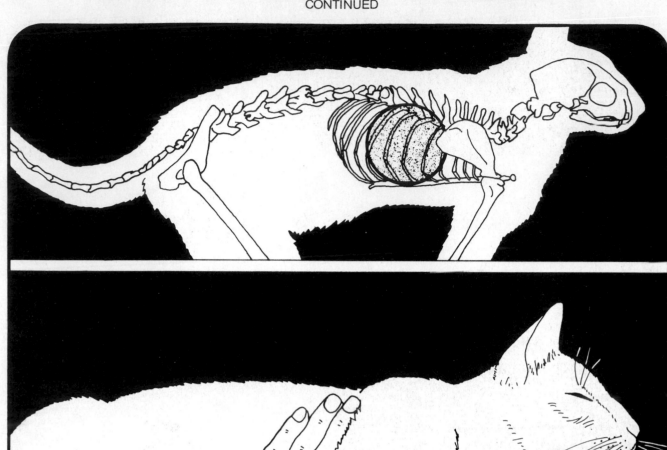

3 **If breathing does not resume:** Compress the rib cage sharply between the palms of your hands at the exact spot shown, then release immediately. **Do not** use excessive force. Look and listen for the air leaving its lungs. If the entry or return of air seems blocked, see **CHOKING,** pages 139-140, then resume artificial respiration. Repeat compressions every 3 seconds for 1 minute, then recheck breathing.

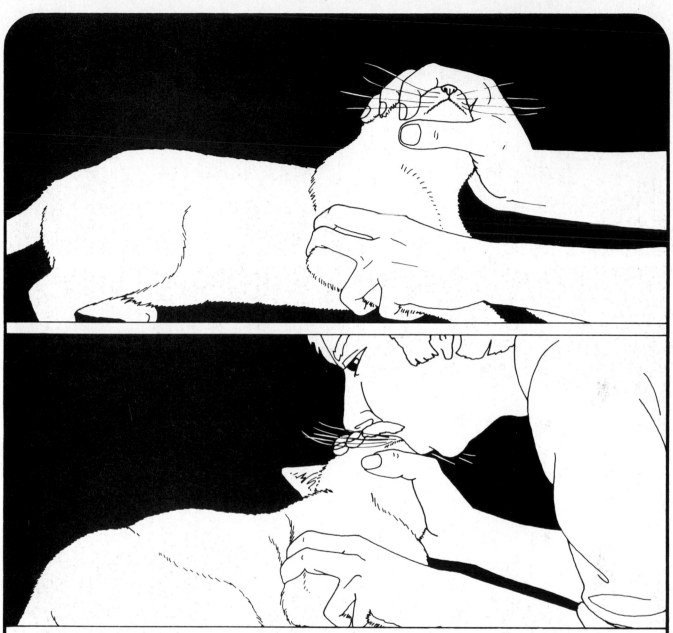

4 **If breathing has not resumed:** Grasp the cat's muzzle firmly and compress the lips and mouth shut. Place your mouth against the cat's nose and blow gently, watching for the chest to rise. If necessary, readjust your hand to seal air leaking from the mouth. Remove your mouth and look and listen for air leaving the cat's lungs. Repeat every 3 seconds for 1 minute, then recheck breathing. Repeat the process until the cat begins to breathe.

BURNS: CHEMICAL

- **Consult your veterinarian as soon as possible.**
- Protect your hands with rubber gloves.

1 **Restrain the cat. See RESTRAINTS, pages 177-185.** Place it immediately under a faucet, hose or other heavy stream of cool water. Remove its collar or harness. Make sure the water reaches the lower layers of fur and the skin. Check the cat's mouth and wash it out if it appears to be red or burned.

2 Soak the fur for 2 minutes, then apply hand soap or gentle shampoo. Lather and rinse well, then repeat the process. Keep the cat under the stream of water for at least 10 minutes, until all traces of the chemical have washed away.

BURNS: CHEMICAL

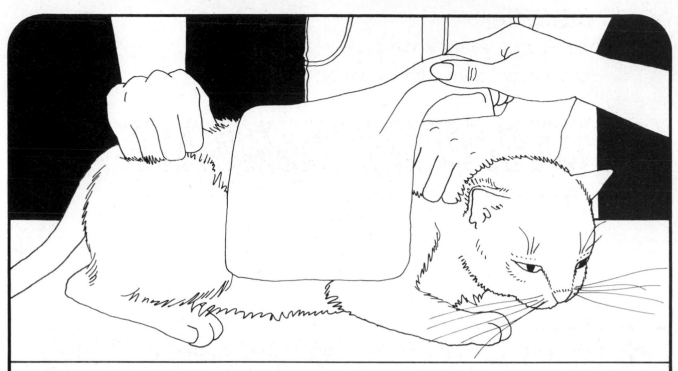

3 Cover the burned skin loosely with a clean, non-adhering dressing or cloth.

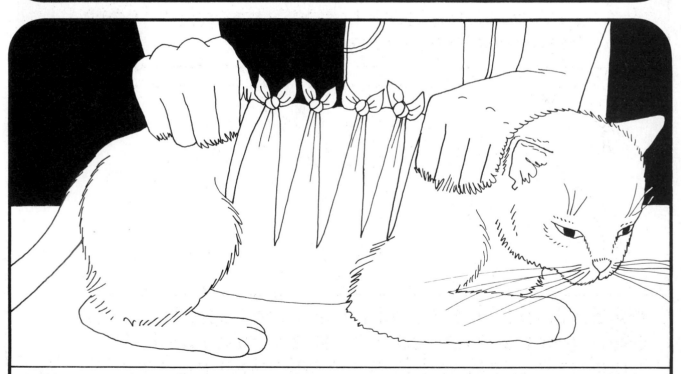

4 Hold the dressing lightly in place with a bandage. Treat for **SHOCK,** pages 170-171.

BURNS: HEAT

1st & 2nd DEGREE

IMPORTANT

- **Do not** remove shreds of tissue or break blisters.
- **Do not** use antiseptic sprays, ointments or home remedies.
- **Do not** put pressure on burned areas.
- Observe for **SHOCK,** pages 170-171.
- **Consult your veterinarian as soon as possible.**

Determine the degree of the burn and treat accordingly.

First Degree: Fur singed or burned off. Red or discolored skin. **See below.**

Second Degree: Fur burned off. Blisters and red or mottled skin. **See below.**

Third Degree: White or charred skin. **See page 138.**

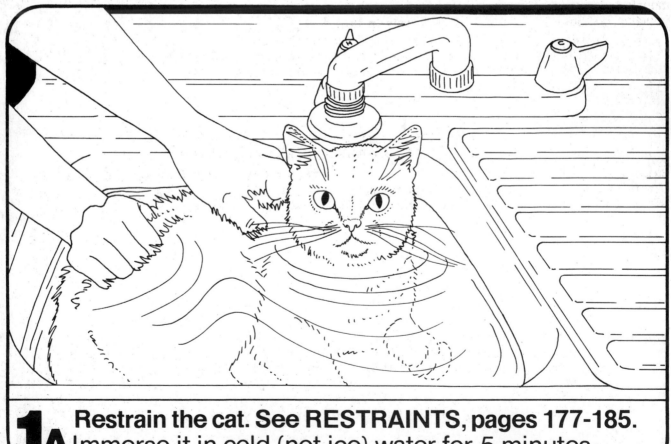

1A **Restrain the cat. See RESTRAINTS, pages 177-185.** Immerse it in cold (not ice) water for 5 minutes.

BURNS: HEAT

1st & 2nd DEGREE

1B Or lightly apply cold clean compresses that have been wrung out after being immersed in ice water.

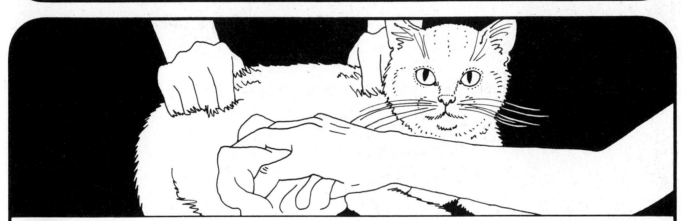

2 Gently blot dry with sterile gauze or a clean cloth.

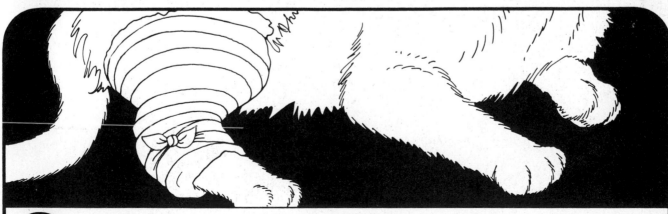

3 Cover loosely with a dry clean dressing.

BURNS: HEAT

3rd DEGREE

➡

IMPORTANT

- **Consult your veterinarian as soon as possible.**

- **Do not** apply water, antiseptic sprays, ointments or home remedies.

- **Do not** remove adhered particles of fur.

- **Do not** remove shreds of tissue or break blisters.

- **Do not** use absorbent cotton.

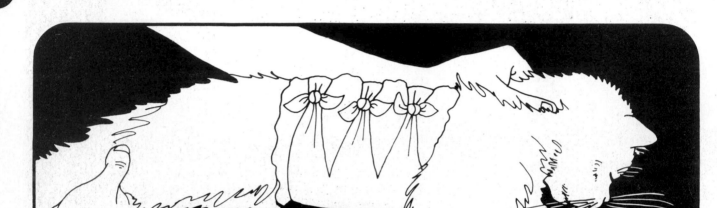

1 **Restrain the cat. See RESTRAINTS, pages 177-185.** Lightly cover the burned area with a nonadhering dressing or a dry, clean cloth.

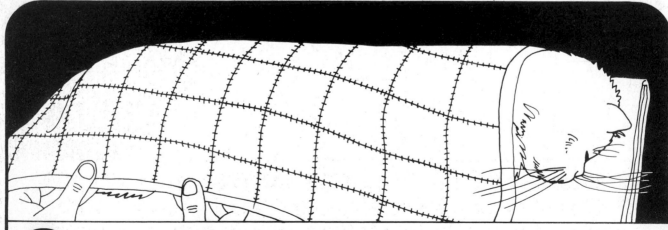

2 Treat for **SHOCK,** pages 170-171.

CHOKING

IMPORTANT

- **Do not** pull thread or string from the cat's throat. A needle or hook may be attached. Get to a veterinarian as soon as possible.

SYMPTOMS

Violent pawing at the face. Gasping and gulping. Great agitation and anxiety.

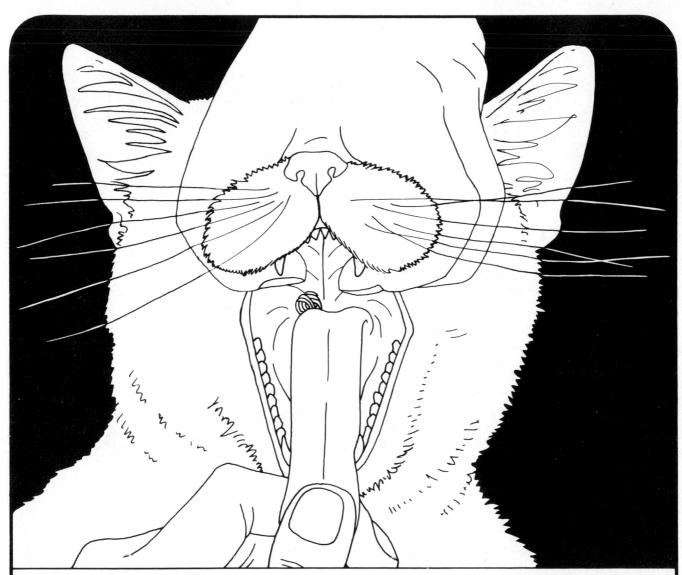

1 **Restrain the cat. See RESTRAINTS, pages 177-185.** Open its mouth wide, and pull out its tongue with your fingers or a cloth. Holding the tongue, look deeply into the cat's throat with a bright light.

CONTINUED ON NEXT PAGE

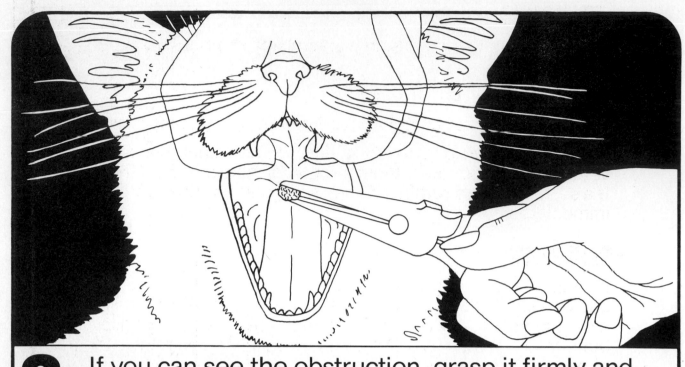

2A If you can see the obstruction, grasp it firmly and gently remove it.

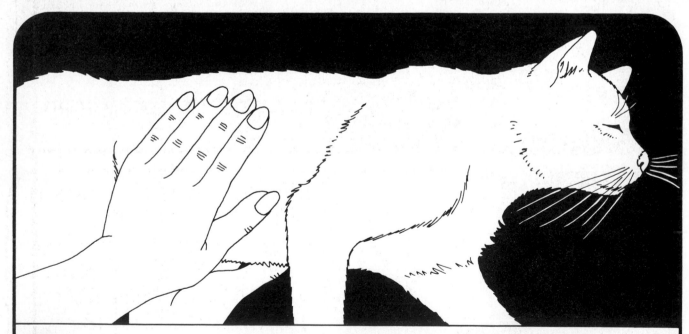

2B If you cannot see the obstruction, lay the cat on its side, place your palms just behind the last rib and give 4 quick thrusts. Recheck the throat. Repeat thrusts if necessary.

CONVULSIONS & SEIZURES

IMPORTANT

- **Do not** handle the cat during a convulsion or for 15 minutes afterward.

- **Do not** try to pull out its tongue.

- **Do not** give the cat anything to drink during the convulsion.

- Although convulsions are rarely fatal unless repetitive, tell your veterinarian about all of them, no matter how brief or infrequent. If a seizure recurs within 2 hours, see your veterinarian immediately.

SYMPTOMS

Falling. Chomping jaws. Stiffening of the body. May void bladder and bowels. Paddling motion of the legs. Jerky, uncontrollable movements, usually lasting 2 to 3 minutes. The cat is conscious but unresponsive. A mild seizure may involve just a short period of body stiffening and confusion.

1 Clear the area of hard or sharp objects that might cause harm. Try to remove its collar or harness, but **do not** restrain the cat.

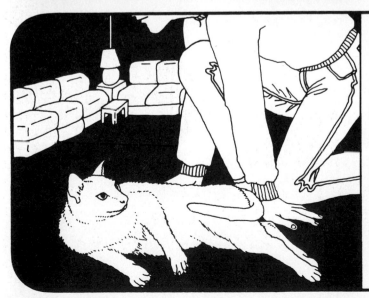

2 When the convulsion subsides, watch breathing closely. If necessary, see **BREATHING: ARTIFICIAL RESPIRATION,** pages 131-133. The cat may show fright and disorientation for 10 to 15 minutes following a seizure.

DIARRHEA

- Consult your veterinarian if the diarrhea contains blood or lasts longer than 24 hours.

- Treat promptly. Diarrhea can seriously dehydrate and weaken the cat.

- Diarrhea can be caused by illness, internal parasites, emotional or environmental factors, or by eating spoiled food or indigestible substances such as hair or grass. It often follows bouts of vomiting within 24 hours.

- To help the veterinarian determine the cause, note if there are worms, grass, mucus or bones in the cat's droppings.

- When the diarrhea has ceased, bring a stool specimen to your veterinarian for analysis.

1 Take the cat's temperature; see **TAKING THE CAT'S TEMPERATURE**, pages 198-199. Consult your veterinarian if it has a fever or shows other symptoms of illness.

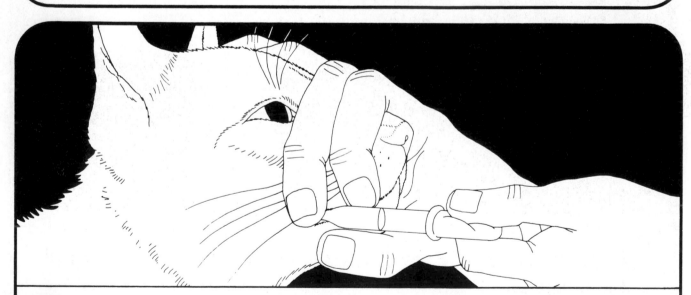

2 If the cat's temperature is normal, withhold food and water and give it 1/2 teaspoon of Pepto-Bismol or Kaopectate every 2 hours for 12 hours; see **ADMINISTERING LIQUID MEDICINE**, page 188. Consult your veterinarian if the cat vomits the medicine.

DIARRHEA

3 After 12 hours, give the cat a small drink of water. If diarrhea does not resume, give it small quantities of water every 3 hours. Consult your veterinarian if diarrhea resumes.

4 After 24 hours, give the cat a small amount of bland food such as cooked hamburger mixed with an equal amount of boiled rice or a cooked egg. Consult your veterinarian if diarrhea resumes. If diarrhea does not resume, repeat small portions of bland food every 3 hours for 24 hours and give normal quantities of water. Continue bland foods in normal portions for 5 days, then return to the cat's regular diet.

DROWNING

IMPORTANT

- **Send for help immediately.**

- **Do not** swim to the cat without a reaching assist. Try to stay at a safe distance. A panicky cat may claw at you.

1A Try to reach the cat from land with a buoy, board or anything that floats.

1B If the cat is too far away to reach, wade in closer with a reaching assist.

144

DROWNING

1c If you must swim to it, keep watching it or the spot you saw it last. Bring something for the cat to cling to or climb on, and pull it to shore.

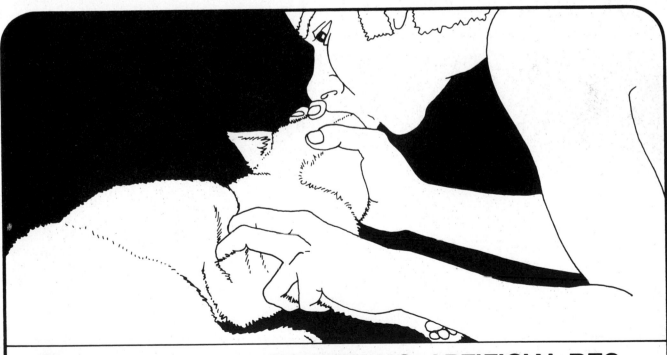

2 If necessary, see **BREATHING: ARTIFICIAL RESPIRATION,** pages 131-133.

EAR INJURIES

- Consult your veterinarian for serious bleeding.

1 **Restrain the cat. See RESTRAINTS, pages 177-185.** Place gauze or a clean cloth behind the cat's ear.

2 Fold the ear over onto the gauze.

146

EAR INJURIES

3 Control the bleeding by pressing the wound against the skull with gauze or a clean cloth.

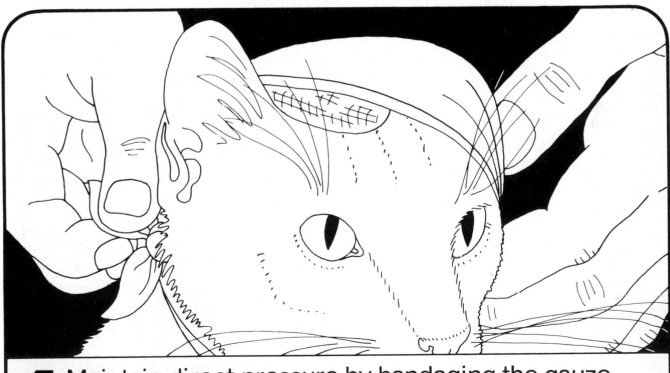

4 Maintain direct pressure by bandaging the gauze firmly in place.

ELECTRIC SHOCK

- **Do not** touch the cat while it remains in contact with the current.

- Suspect electric shock from biting an electrical cord if the cat has red sores in the corners of its mouth; charred lips, gums and teeth; profuse thick salivation; dazed expression. See Step 2 below.

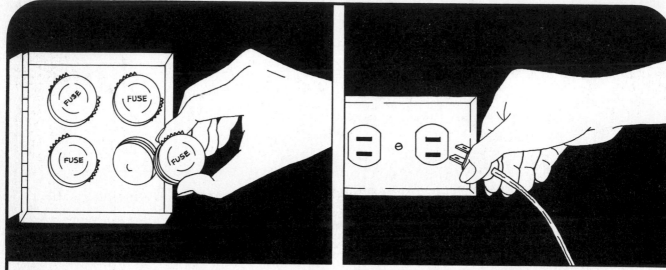

1A Try to turn off the current by removing the fuse or unplugging the electrical cord from the outlet.

1B If that isn't possible, stand on something dry— a blanket, rubber mat, newspapers, etc.—and push the cat away with a dry board or pole.

148

ELECTRIC SHOCK

1c Or pull the cat away with a dry rope looped around one of its legs.

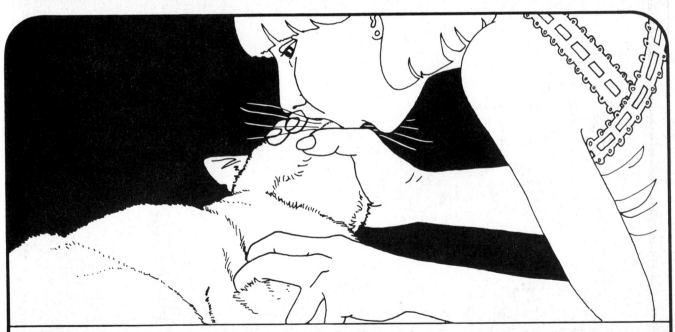

2 If necessary, begin rescue breathing immediately; see **BREATHING: ARTIFICIAL RESPIRATION,** pages 131-133. Treat for **SHOCK,** pages 170-171, and **BURNS,** pages 136-138. **Consult your veterinarian.**

EYE INJURIES

CHEMICALS IN THE EYE

IMPORTANT

- Be aware that the cat has an opaque third eyelid which is not normally seen but may come up to protect an injured eye. Should this happen, **do not** try to remove it or otherwise interfere with it.

1 **Restrain the cat. See RESTRAINTS, pages 177-185.** Holding the eyelid open, flush the eye immediately with gently running water for up to 2 minutes. **Do not** let the water run into the other eye.

2 Apply gauze or a clean cloth. Hold it in place with a loosely fastened bandage. **Consult your veterinarian as soon as possible.**

EYE INJURIES
FOREIGN OBJECTS

- Be aware that the cat has an opaque third eyelid which is not normally seen but may come up to protect an injured eye. Should this happen, **do not** try to remove it or otherwise interfere with it.

1 **Restrain the cat. See RESTRAINTS, pages 177-185.** Facing the cat, grasp the lower lid between your thumb and index finger and gently pull it away from the eyeball. If you cannot see the object, grasp the upper lid and elevate the head to expose the upper surface of the eye.

CONTINUED ON NEXT PAGE

EYE INJURIES

FOREIGN OBJECTS

CONTINUED

2A For a small foreign object, wash out the eye with water, letting the water drain down and away from the eye.

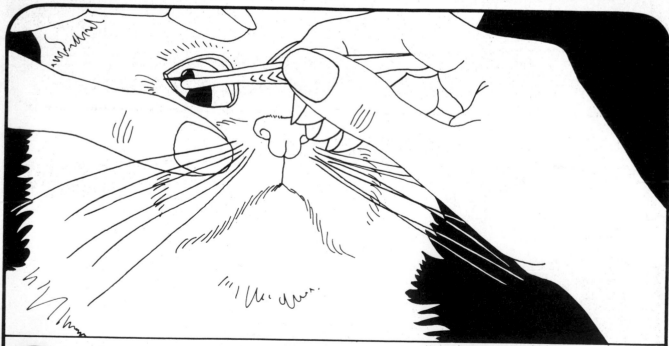

2B Carefully use blunt tweezers to remove thorns, etc. that cling to the surface of the eye or the lid.

EYE INJURIES

EYELID, EYEBALL & IMPALED OBJECTS

- **Consult your veterinarian as soon as possible.**

- **Restrain the cat before administering first aid. See RESTRAINTS, pages 177-185.**

- **Do not** wash out the eye.

- Be aware that the cat has an opaque third eyelid which is not normally seen but may come up to protect an injured eye. Should this happen, **do not** try to remove it or otherwise interfere with it.

LACERATED EYELID

Control the bleeding by applying direct pressure against the lid and bone with gauze or a clean cloth.

LACERATED EYEBALL

Cover **both** eyes loosely with gauze or a clean cloth. **Do not** apply pressure.

CONTINUED ON NEXT PAGE

EYE INJURIES
EYELID, EYEBALL & IMPALED OBJECTS
CONTINUED

IMPALED OBJECTS

NOTE: Try to remove the object if it is sharp, smooth and straight. It is better not to transport the cat with an impaled object still in its eye, but if the object cannot be removed, follow Step 3 only.

1 Using great gentleness and care, remove the object with your fingers, tweezers, needlenose pliers, etc.

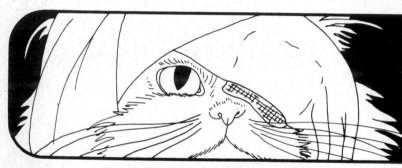

2 Apply gauze or a clean cloth and hold it in place with a loosely fastened bandage.

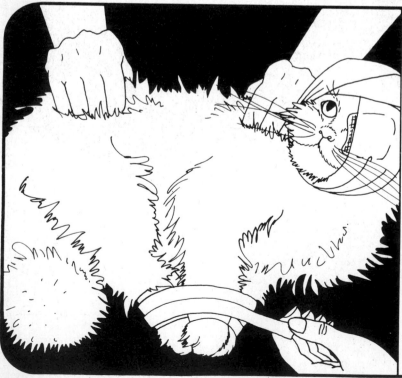

3 Bind the front paws together by wrapping adhesive tape around them twice. Immobilize the hind paws the same way, then bind the front and hind paws together. **Take the cat to the veterinarian immediately.** See **TRANSPORTING AN INJURED CAT,** pages 172-173.

FISHHOOKS

IMPORTANT

- **Do not** attempt to remove a fishhook in or near the cat's eye. **Consult your veterinarian immediately.**

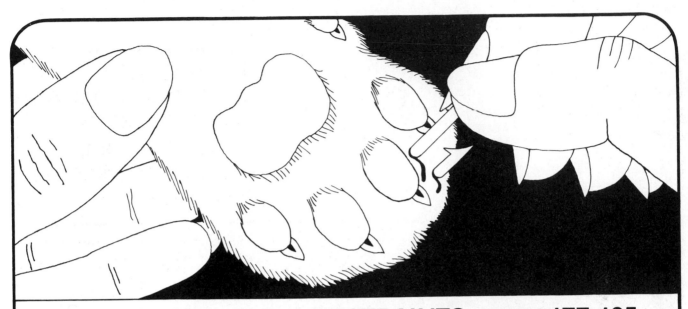

1 **Restrain the cat. See RESTRAINTS, pages 177-185.** Push the shank through the skin until the point appears.

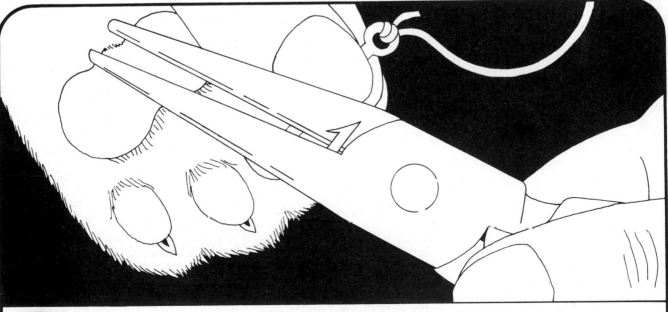

2 Cut off the barbed end with clippers or pliers.

CONTINUED ON NEXT PAGE

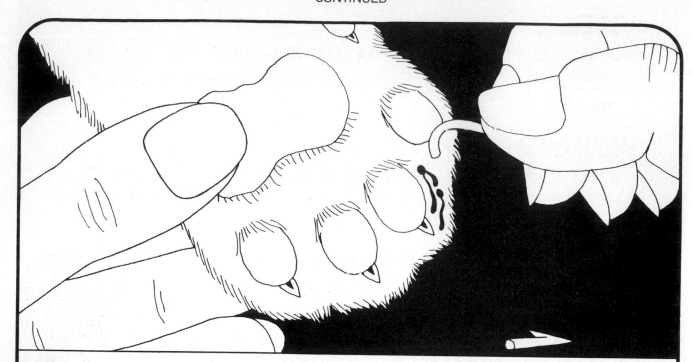

3 Remove the shank from the wound. Encourage bleeding.

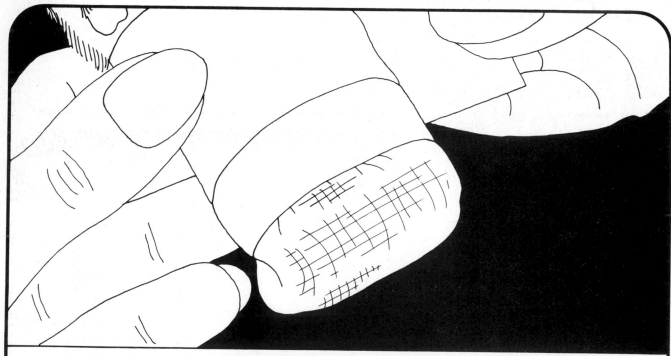

4 Wash the wound with soap and water and apply "tamed" iodine or other antiseptic. Cover with gauze or a clean cloth. **Consult your veterinarian.**

HEART FAILURE

IMPORTANT

- **Consult your veterinarian as soon as possible.**

- Waste no time, but be certain all symptoms are present before beginning first aid.

SYMPTOMS

Unconsciousness. No breathing. No heartbeat can be felt when you gently squeeze the lower third of the cat's chest between your thumb and fingers.

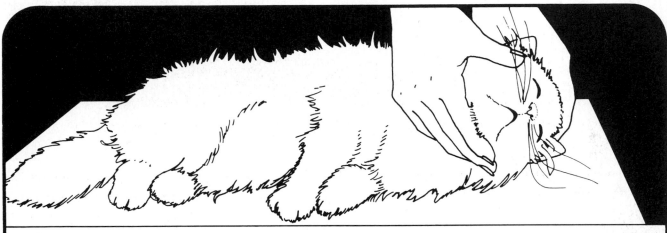

1 Place the cat on its side with its head extended. Remove its collar or harness.

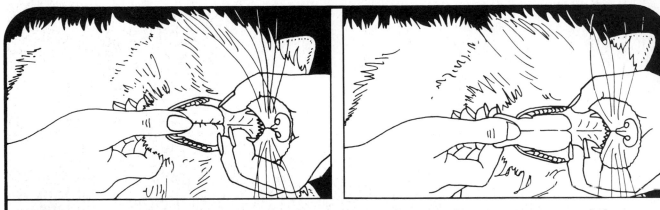

2 Open the cat's mouth and pull out its tongue with your fingers or a cloth. Hold the tongue to keep the airway open. If necessary, clear out its mouth with your fingers or a cloth.

CONTINUED ON NEXT PAGE

3 Recheck all symptoms. If the heartbeat has not resumed, quickly and firmly compress the lower third of the cat's chest between your thumb and fingers at the exact spot shown. Release immediately. **Do not** bring your fingers closer together than 1 inch. Repeat once a second for 1 minute.

4 Recheck all symptoms again. If the heartbeat still has not resumed, repeat Step 3. When heartbeat resumes, begin rescue breathing; see **BREATHING: ARTIFICIAL RESPIRATION,** pages 131-133.

HEATSTROKE

IMPORTANT

- **Consult your veterinarian as soon as possible.**

- Act quickly. Body temperature must be immediately lowered to 103°F. (39.4°C.). See **TAKING THE CAT'S TEMPERATURE,** pages 198-199.

- Watch temperature closely; repeat first aid if it rises again.

- Watch breathing closely. If necessary, see **BREATHING: ARTIFICIAL RESPIRATION,** pages 131-133.

SYMPTOMS

Extremely high body temperature (105°F.—110°F.; 40.6°C.—43.3°C.). Uncontrollable panting. Foaming at the mouth. Depression. Agitation. Loss of consciousness. Tongue and gums become progressively blue or gray.

1A Bathe or hose the cat with cold water until temperature subsides.

CONTINUED ON NEXT PAGE

HEATSTROKE

1B Or take the cat to a cool, well-ventilated place and wrap it in a wet, cold sheet or towel until temperature subsides.

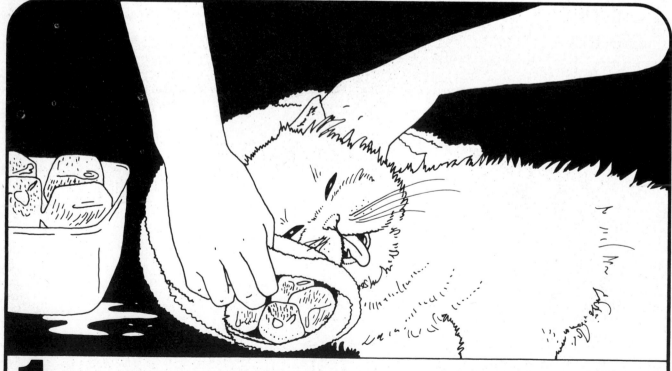

1C Or pack the cat's head in ice until it stops panting.

MOUTH INJURIES
GUMS, PALATE, TEETH, LIPS & TONGUE

IMPORTANT

- **Restrain the cat before administering first aid.** See **RESTRAINTS,** pages 177-185.

- Cautiously clear the mouth of broken teeth.

- Keep the cat sitting up with its head lowered slightly so it does not inhale blood.

- **Do not** treat mouth injuries if the cat is vicious. Consult your veterinarian immediately.

GUMS & PALATE

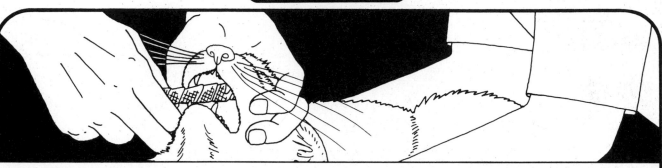

Control bleeding by direct pressure with gauze pads or a clean cloth wrapped around a tongue depressor, spoon, tweezers, etc.

TEETH

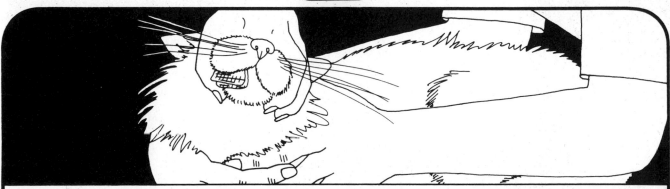

Control bleeding by direct pressure on the tooth socket with gauze pads or a clean cloth. Hold the mouth shut so the cat bites down firmly on the gauze to keep it in place.

CONTINUED ON NEXT PAGE

MOUTH INJURIES

GUMS, PALATE, TEETH, LIPS & TONGUE
CONTINUED

LIPS

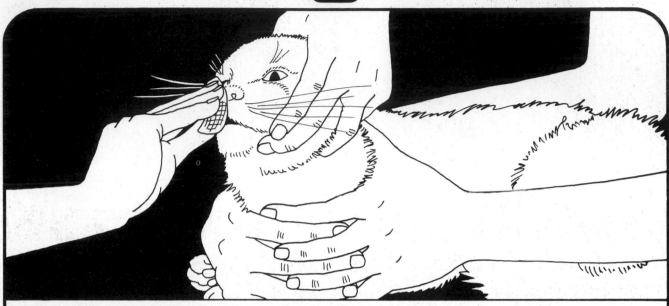

Upper Lip: Put a gauze pad or clean cloth directly over the wound. Place your thumb on the lip behind the wound and your other fingers over the pad, then apply direct pressure by squeezing your fingers together.

Lower Lip: Control bleeding by pressing gauze pads or a clean cloth directly on the wound.

MOUTH INJURIES

GUMS, PALATE, TEETH, LIPS & TONGUE

TONGUE

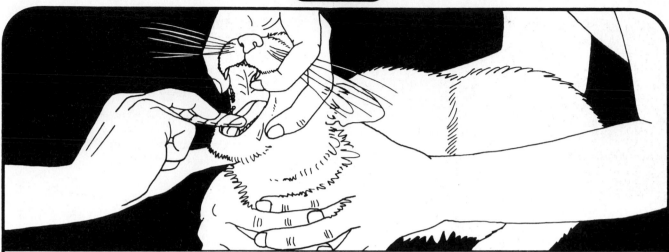

If the cat is conscious: Apply direct pressure with several gauze pads wrapped around a tongue depressor, spoon, etc. held in place with your index and middle fingers. Apply counterpressure by placing your thumb behind the chin and pressing up firmly.

If the cat is unconscious: Prop the jaws apart by placing a small block of wood or the like between the teeth at the back of the mouth. Control bleeding by pressing both sides of the tongue with gauze or a clean cloth. For more severe bleeding, gently pull the tongue and hold it for about 5 minutes.

POISONING

CONTACT

IMPORTANT

- **Consult your veterinarian if there is a severe reaction or if the cat is highly allergic.**

- Burns on the mouth could indicate **ELECTRIC SHOCK,** pages 148-149, or **SWALLOWED POISONS,** pages 168-169.

- Watch breathing closely. If necessary, see **BREATHING: ARTIFICIAL RESPIRATION,** pages 131-133.

- **Do not** use chemical solvents unless your veterinarian so advises.

- Contact poisoning is frequently caused by treating the cat with a parasite bath in combination with a flea collar. It can also be caused by using a dog parasite bath on a cat.

SYMPTOMS

Burns. Vomiting. Profuse salivation. Swelling. Fever. Convulsive seizures (usually occur within 24 hours after contact with such toxic substances as poisons, oil, gasoline, turpentine, benzine and chemical dips).

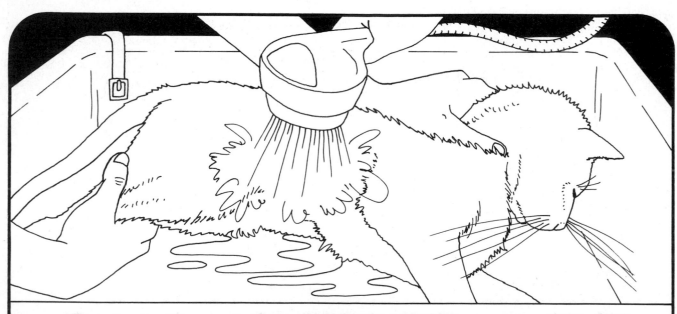

1 **Restrain the cat. See RESTRAINTS, pages 177-185.** Remove its collar or harness. Bathe or hose the cat with lukewarm water.

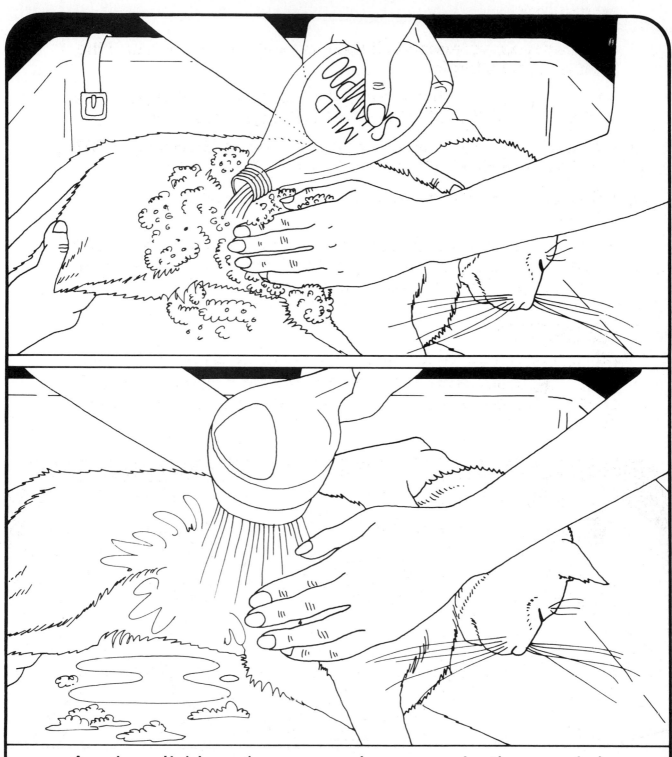

2 Apply mild hand soap or shampoo. Lather and rinse well. Repeat the process until all traces of the toxic substance have washed away.

POISONING

INGESTED PLANTS

IMPORTANT

- **Call your veterinarian or Poison Control Center immediately.**

- Cats rarely ingest poisonous plants. **Do not** treat for poisoning unless you have witnessed the poisoning or are certain that poison is involved.

- Watch breathing closely. If necessary, see **BREATHING: ARTIFICIAL RESPIRATION,** pages 131-133.

- **Do not** give the cat anything to drink if it is unconscious.

- **If you cannot reach your veterinarian or Poison Control Center, see POISONING: SWALLOWED POISONS, page 169, and follow treatment Ⓑ .**

COMMON POISONOUS PLANTS

BANEBERRY

BITTERSWEET

CASTOR-OIL PLANT

DAPHNE

FOXGLOVE

POISONING

INGESTED PLANTS

JIMSON WEED

LARKSPUR

LILY-OF-THE-VALLEY

MONKSHOOD

NIGHTSHADE

POISON HEMLOCK

POKEWEED

WATER HEMLOCK

YEW

POISONING
SWALLOWED POISONS

IMPORTANT

- **Call your veterinarian or Poison Control Center immediately.**

- Poisoning is relatively rare in cats. **Do not** treat for poisoning unless you have witnessed the poisoning or are certain that poison is involved.

- Burns on the mouth could also indicate **ELECTRIC SHOCK**; see pages 148-149.

- Save the poison container and a sample of the vomit.

- Watch breathing closely. If necessary, see **BREATHING: ARTIFICIAL RESPIRATION,** pages 131-133.

- **Do not** give the cat anything to drink if it is unconscious.

If you cannot reach your veterinarian or Poison Control Center:

- Find the poison swallowed on the list below.

- Follow the corresponding treatment on the opposite page.

- If you don't know what was swallowed, follow treatment **Ⓐ**. If there are no burns around the mouth, also have the cat drink 1 heaping teaspoon of activated charcoal mixed in 1 ounce of water. See **ADMINISTERING LIQUID MEDICINE,** page 188.

Acetone Ⓑ	Fingernail Polish & Remover Ⓑ	Naphtha Ⓐ
After Shave Lotion Ⓑ	Fireworks Ⓑ	Oil of Wintergreen Ⓑ
Alcohol Ⓑ	Floor Polish Ⓐ	Oven Cleaner Ⓐ
Antifreeze Ⓑ	Fluoride Ⓑ	Paint (Lead) Ⓑ
Arsenic Ⓑ	Furniture Polish Ⓐ	Paint Thinner Ⓐ
Battery Acid Ⓐ	Gasoline Ⓐ	Perfume Ⓑ
Benzine Ⓑ	Grease Remover Ⓐ	Pesticides Ⓑ
Bichloride of Mercury Ⓑ	Gun Cleaner Ⓐ	Pine Oil Ⓑ
Bleach Ⓑ	Hair Dye Ⓑ	Quicklime Ⓐ
Body Conditioner Ⓑ	Hair Permanent Neutralizer Ⓑ	Rat or Mouse Poison Ⓑ
Boric Acid Ⓑ	Hair Preparations Ⓑ	Roach Poison Ⓑ
Brush Cleaner Ⓐ	Hydrogen Peroxide Ⓑ	Shoe Polish Ⓐ
Camphor Ⓑ	Indelible Markers Ⓑ	Strychnine Ⓑ
Carbon Tetrachloride Ⓑ	Ink (Green & Purple) Ⓑ	Suntan Preparations Ⓑ
Charcoal Lighter Ⓐ	Insecticides Ⓑ	Toilet Bowl Cleaner Ⓐ
Chlordane Ⓑ	Iodine Ⓑ	Turpentine Ⓑ
Cologne Ⓑ	Kerosene Ⓐ	Typewriter Cleaner Ⓐ
Corn Remover Ⓐ	Lacquer Thinner Ⓐ	Wart Remover Ⓐ
Cosmetics Ⓑ	Liniment Ⓑ	Washing Soda Ⓐ
DDT Ⓑ	Lye Ⓐ	Wax (Floor or Furniture) Ⓐ
Deodorant Ⓑ	Matches (more than 20 wooden matches	Weed Killer Ⓑ
Detergent Ⓑ	or 2 match books) Ⓑ	Wick Deodorizer Ⓑ
Dishwasher Granules Ⓐ	Mercury Salts Ⓑ	Wood Preservative Ⓐ
Drain Cleaner Ⓐ	Metal Cleaner Ⓐ	Zinc Compounds Ⓐ
Fabric Softeners Ⓑ	Mothballs, Flakes or Cakes Ⓑ	

POISONING
SWALLOWED POISONS

A FOR ACID, ALKALI & PETROLEUM POISONING

IMPORTANT

• **Do not induce vomiting.**

SYMPTOMS OF ACID & ALKALI POISONING Burns around the mouth, lips and tongue.

SYMPTOMS OF PETROLEUM POISONING Coughing. Petroleum odor on the breath. Bloody vomit. Coma.

1 **Restrain the cat. See RESTRAINTS, pages 177-185.**
If the cat is conscious, give it 1 cup of milk (or as much as it will accept) to dilute the poison. (If milk isn't available, use water.) See **ADMINISTERING LIQUID MEDICINE,** page 188.

2 Observe for **SHOCK,** pages 170-171.

B FOR OTHER POISONING

SYMPTOMS May include vomiting, pain, lack of coordination, panting, slimy mouth, convulsions, coma.

1 **Restrain the cat. See RESTRAINTS, pages 177-185.**
If the cat is conscious, give it 1 cup of milk (or as much as it will accept) to dilute the poison. (If milk isn't available, use water.) See **ADMINISTERING LIQUID MEDICINE,** page 188.

2 Induce vomiting by giving the cat 1 teaspoon 3% medicinal hydrogen peroxide U.S.P. or 1/2 teaspoon table salt in 1 tablespoon of water. If it doesn't vomit within 30 minutes, give it a second dose.

3 When the cat has finished vomiting, give it 1 heaping teaspoon of activated charcoal mixed in 1 ounce of water.

4 Observe for **SHOCK,** pages 170-171.

SHOCK

IMPORTANT

- **Always check a seriously injured cat for shock.**
- **Consult your veterinarian as soon as possible.**
- **Do not** give the cat anything to drink.

SYMPTOMS

Weak or rapid but shallow breathing. Confusion. Pale gums. Weakness. Semiconsciousness or unconsciousness.

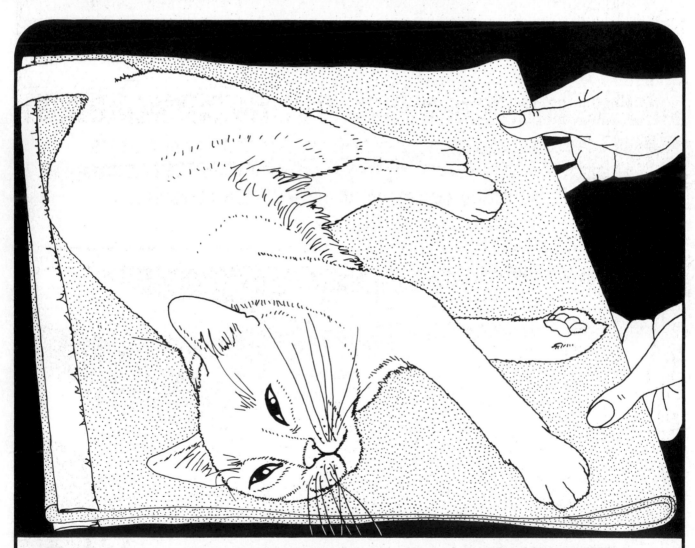

1 **Restrain the cat if necessary. See RESTRAINTS, pages 177-185.** Place the cat on its side with its head extended. Put a blanket or jacket under it if it is cold or damp.

SHOCK

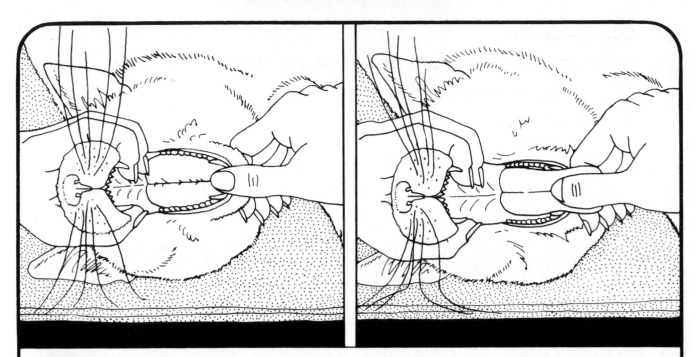

2 Open the cat's mouth and cautiously pull out its tongue with your fingers or a cloth. Hold the tongue to keep the airway open. If the cat is unconscious, elevate its hindquarters slightly.

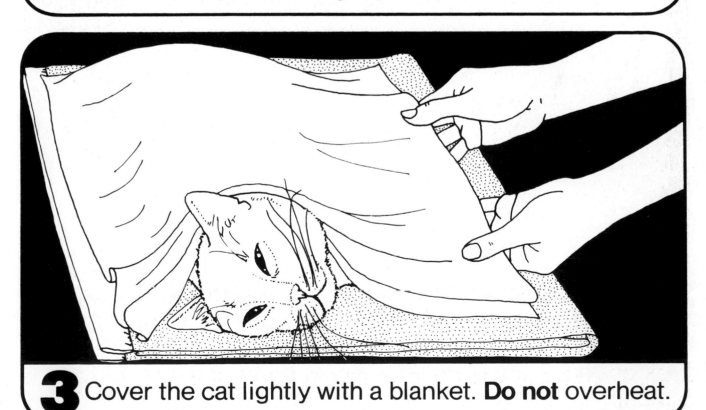

3 Cover the cat lightly with a blanket. **Do not** overheat.

TRANSPORTING A CAT

- **Always approach an injured cat with caution.** Speak in a gentle, reassuring voice. If possible, protect your hands with gloves.

- If the cat is unconscious or paralyzed, lift it carefully as a single unit, without bending or twisting any part of its body, and place it in a cat carrier or other container.

- If possible, call ahead to the veterinarian.

1 Grasp the cat by the scruff of the head and neck.

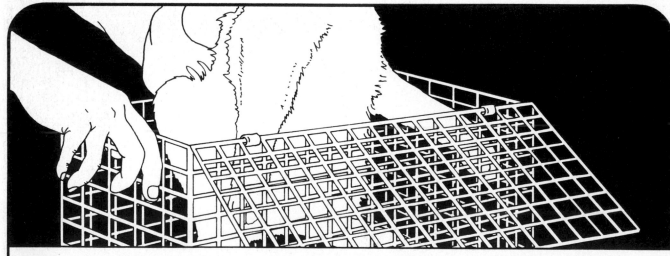

2A Lift it straight up and place it down inside a cat carrier, box or other closed container, then close the top.

TRANSPORTING A CAT

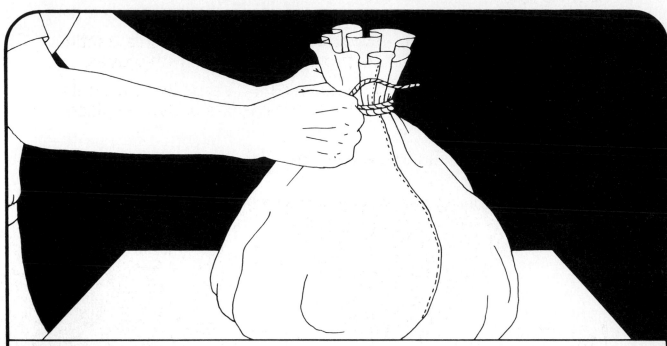

2B Or place it in a pillowcase or sack, and tie the top closed.

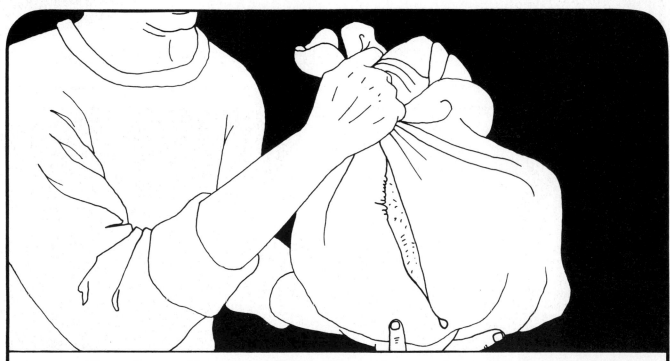

2c Or place it on a blanket or large towel, then gather the corners together to form a closed sack. Fasten securely with string or adhesive tape.

VOMITING

IMPORTANT

- Vomiting can be caused by illness, emotional or environmental factors, or by eating spoiled food or indigestible substances such as hair and grass.

- Consult your veterinarian if the vomit contains blood or if vomiting occurs frequently, lasts longer than several hours or the cat seems otherwise ill or in pain.

1 Take the cat's temperature; see **TAKING THE CAT'S TEMPERATURE,** pages 198-199. Consult your veterinarian if it has a fever or shows other symptoms of illness.

2 If the cat's temperature is normal, withhold food and water and give it 1/2 teaspoon of Pepto-Bismol or Kaopectate every 2 hours for 12 hours; see **ADMINISTERING LIQUID MEDICINE,** page 188. Consult your veterinarian if the cat vomits the medicine.

VOMITING

3 After 12 hours, give the cat a small drink of water. If it does not vomit, give it small quantities of water every 3 hours. Consult your veterinarian if the cat does not drink any water or vomits after drinking.

4 After 24 hours, give the cat a small amount of bland food such as cooked hamburger mixed with an equal amount of boiled rice or a cooked egg. If the cat still does not vomit, repeat small portions of water and food every 3 hours for 24 hours. Continue bland foods in normal portions for 3 days, then return to the cat's regular diet.

RESTRAINTS

RESTRAINTS

IF YOU HAVE ASSISTANCE AND THE CAT IS COOPERATIVE

IMPORTANT

- Always approach an injured cat with caution. Speak in a gentle, reassuring voice. If possible, protect your hands with gloves.

- If possible, perform all restraints on a smooth tabletop or other elevated surface.

- An injured cat that is still conscious should always be restrained before it receives first aid.

- Whenever possible, have someone restrain the cat for you while you administer the emergency treatment. See **AIDED RESTRAINTS** below.

- If you cannot obtain assistance and the cat is unconscious, requires medication or has a head injury, use the **UNAIDED RESTRAINT** on pages 182-183.

- For all other emergencies, use the **EMERGENCY RESTRAINT** on pages 183-185.

- If the cat is uncooperative or vicious, use the **EMERGENCY RESTRAINT** on pages 183-185.

AIDED RESTRAINT A FOR ADMINISTERING MEDICINE & TREATING THE HEAD

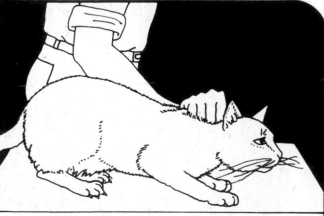

1 Tell your assistant to grasp the cat by the scruff of the head and neck, lift it straight up and place it down on its chest with its back toward him.

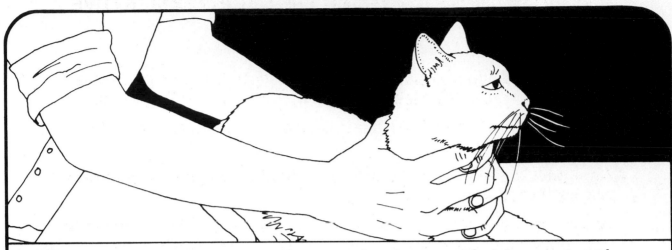

2 Have him release the neck, then quickly grasp the upper part of the front legs from behind and firmly press down the front feet and chest so the cat cannot raise its paws. Tell him to keep his forearms pressed along the cat's body. Proceed to administer the appropriate first aid.

AIDED RESTRAINT B
FOR TAKING TEMPERATURE & TREATING THE BACK END EXCEPT FOR THE LEGS

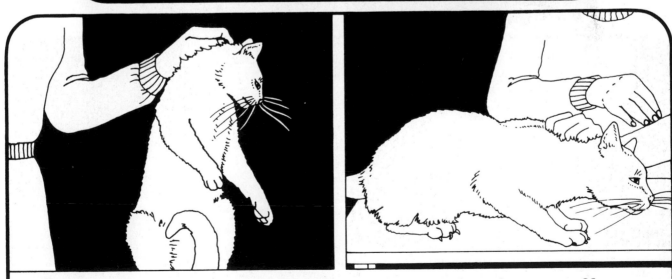

1 Tell your assistant to grasp the cat by the scruff of the head and neck, and place it down on its chest.

CONTINUED ON NEXT PAGE

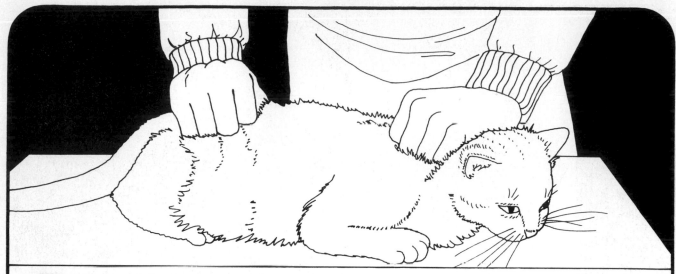

2 Have him grasp the loose skin of the neck with one hand and the loose skin of the back with the other hand, then press the cat down firmly with both hands so it cannot raise its paws. Proceed to administer the appropriate first aid.

AIDED RESTRAINT C
FOR TREATING THE LEGS, SIDE & TAIL AREA

1 Tell your assistant to grasp the cat by the scruff of the head and neck, and lift it straight up.

RESTRAINTS

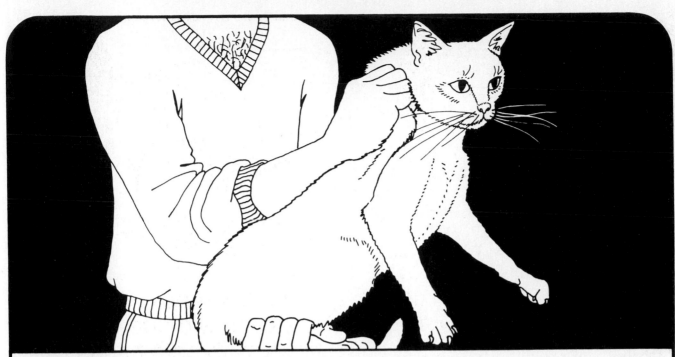

2 Have him grasp the rear paws or legs with his other hand and extend the cat's body fully.

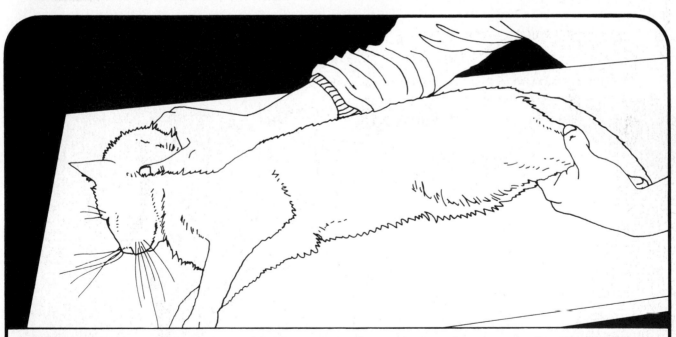

3 Tell him to place the cat down on its uninjured side with its body extended, then press it down firmly against the table. Proceed to administer the appropriate first aid.

181

RESTRAINTS

IF YOU ARE ALONE OR THE CAT IS UNCOOPERATIVE OR VICIOUS

IMPORTANT

- Always approach an injured cat with caution. Speak in a gentle, reassuring voice. If possible, protect your hands with gloves.

- An injured cat that is still conscious should always be restrained before it receives first aid.

- Whenever possible, have someone restrain the cat for you while you administer the emergency treatment. See **AIDED RE-STRAINTS,** pages 178-181.

- If you cannot obtain assistance:

  - •• If the cat is unconscious, requires medication or has a head injury, see **UNAIDED RESTRAINT** below.

  - •• For all other emergencies or for an uncooperative or vicious cat, see **EMERGENCY RESTRAINT,** pages 183-185.

UNAIDED RESTRAINT
FOR ADMINISTERING MEDICINE & TREATING THE HEAD

1 Grasp the cat by the scruff of the head and neck, lift it straight up and place it down on its chest on a smooth tabletop or other elevated surface.

RESTRAINTS

2 Tip the head all the way back while pushing the cat down firmly with the heel of your hand and wrist. Administer the appropriate first aid with your other hand.

EMERGENCY RESTRAINT
FOR ALL OTHER EMERGENCIES OR FOR AN UNCOOPERATIVE OR VICIOUS CAT

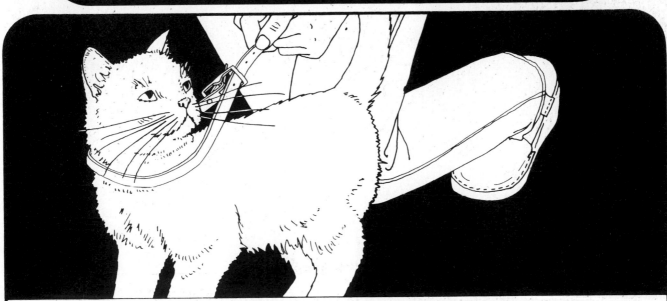

1 Improvise a noose from a length of rope, a belt, etc. and slip it cautiously over the cat's neck.

CONTINUED ON NEXT PAGE

RESTRAINTS

2 Tighten the noose gently and pass the free end through a fence or other fixed object.

3 Pull the cat against the fixed object and secure the rope so the cat cannot effectively move. If the cat is tranquil, tie the end to free both your hands.

4 Cautiously grasp the rear legs and extend the cat's body so it cannot reach you with its claws. Take care not to choke the cat. (If necessary, bind the front paws together by wrapping adhesive tape around them twice. Immobilize the hind paws the same way.)

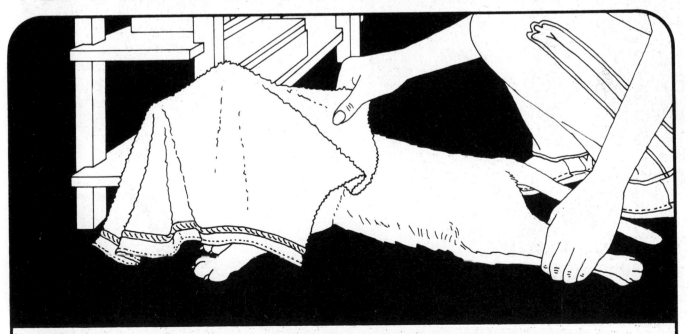

5 Calm the cat by covering its head with a towel or cloth. Proceed to administer the appropriate first aid.

ADMINISTERING MEDICINE AND TAKING THE CAT'S TEMPERATURE

ADMINISTERING LIQUID MEDICINE

IMPORTANT

- Be gentle but firm and decisive. Speak in a quiet, reassuring voice.
- Administer liquid slowly to keep it from being coughed out or inhaled.

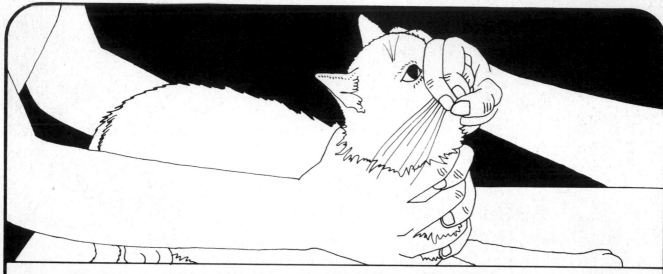

1 **Restrain the cat. See RESTRAINTS, pages 177-185.** Holding the cat's mouth shut, gently tip back its head very slightly.

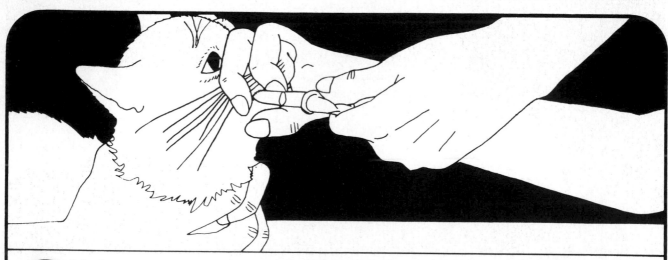

2 Using a plastic eyedropper or dosing syringe, slowly feed the medicine between the molar and canine teeth at the side of the mouth. **Do not** clamp the jaws shut; the cat must move its tongue to swallow.

ADMINISTERING PILLS

- Be gentle but firm and decisive. Speak in a quiet, reassuring voice.
- Lubricate capsules or large pills with butter before administering.

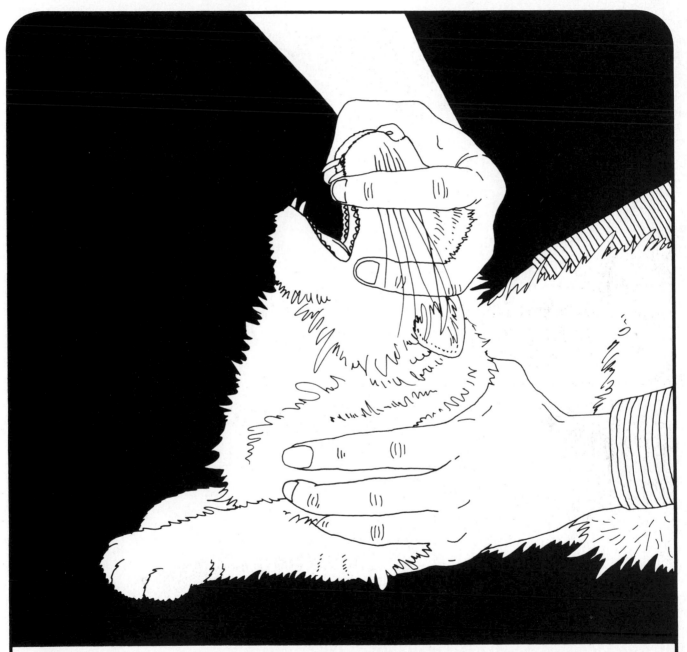

1 **Restrain the cat. See RESTRAINTS, pages 177-185.** Place one hand behind the cat's head and over its eyes, with your thumb and index finger just behind the long fang teeth. Tip the head all the way back.

CONTINUED ON NEXT PAGE

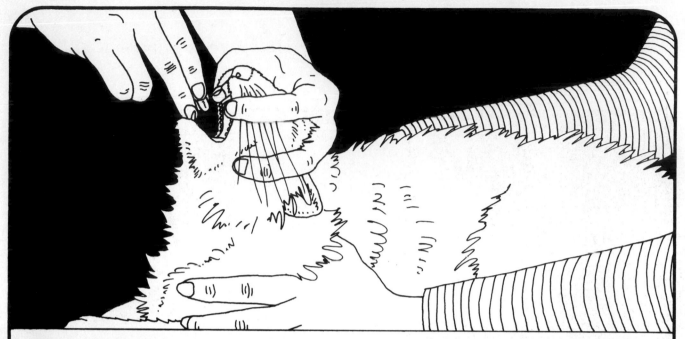

2 Hold the pill between the thumb and index finger of your other hand. Use your middle finger to hold the cat's mouth wide open, and drop the pill as far back in the throat as possible.

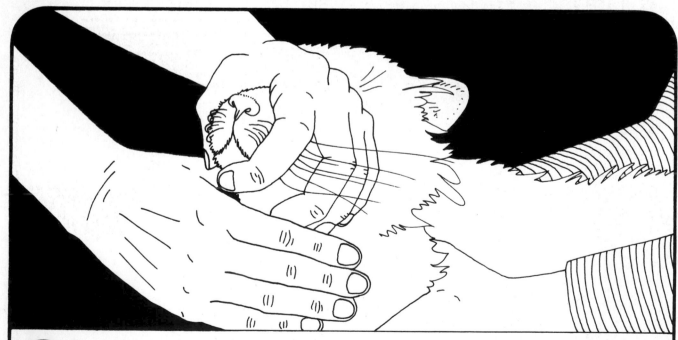

3 Quickly close the cat's mouth and lower its head to a level position. Stroke its throat to stimulate swallowing.

190

APPLYING MEDICINE TO THE EARS

- **Do not** put medicine in the cat's ears unless your veterinarian recommends it.

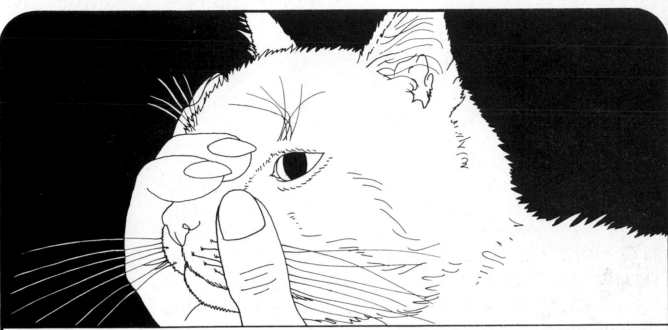

1 **Restrain the cat. See RESTRAINTS, pages 177-185.** Grasp the cat's muzzle and steady its head.

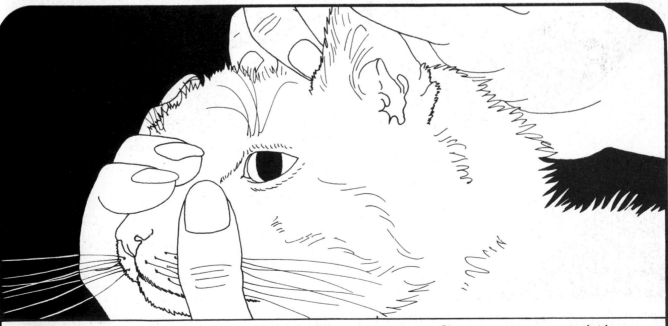

2 Using your other hand, fold the ear flap up toward the head.

CONTINUED ON NEXT PAGE

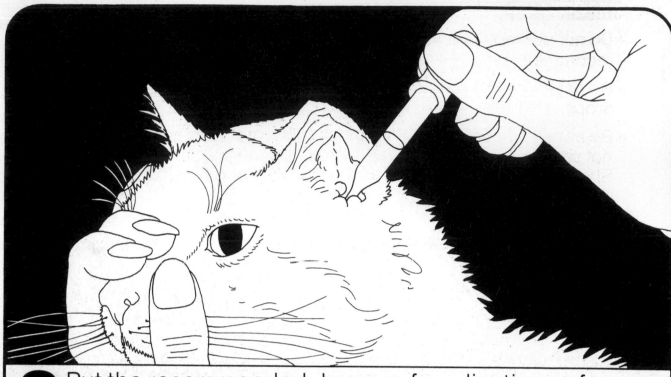

3 Put the recommended dosage of medication as far into the ear canal as you can see.

4 Massage the area outside and under the ear opening to distribute the medication.

APPLYING LIQUID MEDICINE TO THE EYES

- **Do not** put medicine in the cat's eyes unless your veterinarian recommends it.

- **Do not** touch the eyeball with the applicator when applying the drops.

- Be aware that cats have an opaque third eyelid which normally is not seen but may come up to protect an irritated or injured eye. Should this happen, **do not** try to remove it or otherwise interfere with it.

1 **Restrain the cat. See RESTRAINTS, pages 177-185.** Place one hand under the cat's jaw, then lift it to elevate the head.

CONTINUED ON NEXT PAGE

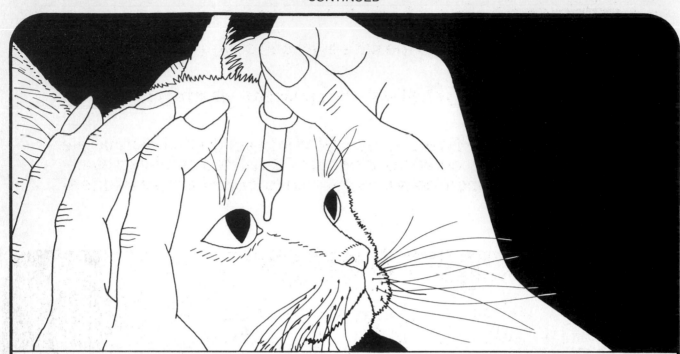

2 Steady the heel of your other hand against the cat's head, then carefully approach the inside corner of the eye with the eyedropper.

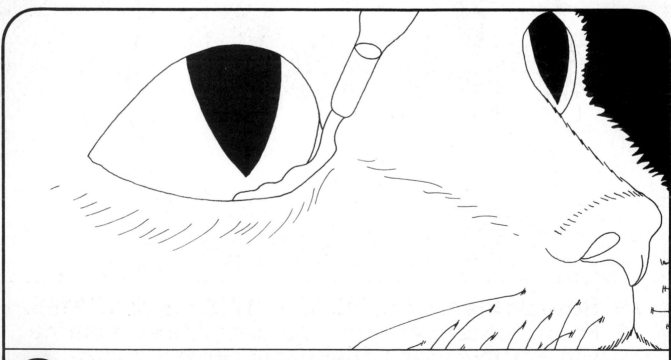

3 Apply the recommended dosage to the eye.

APPLYING OINTMENT TO THE EYES

- **Do not** put medicine in the cat's eyes unless your veterinarian recommends it.

- **Do not** touch the eyeball with the applicator when applying the ointment.

- Be aware that cats have an opaque third eyelid which normally is not seen but may come up to protect an irritated or injured eye. Should this happen, **do not** try to remove it or otherwise interfere with it.

1 **Restrain the cat. See RESTRAINTS, pages 177-185.** Facing the cat, gently pull the lower lid away from the eye with your thumb and index finger. Hold the eyelid open.

CONTINUED ON NEXT PAGE

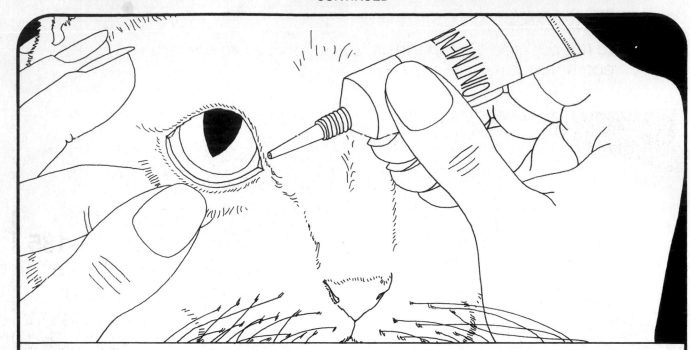

2 Steady the heel of your other hand against the cat's head, then carefully approach the inside corner of the eye with the ointment tube.

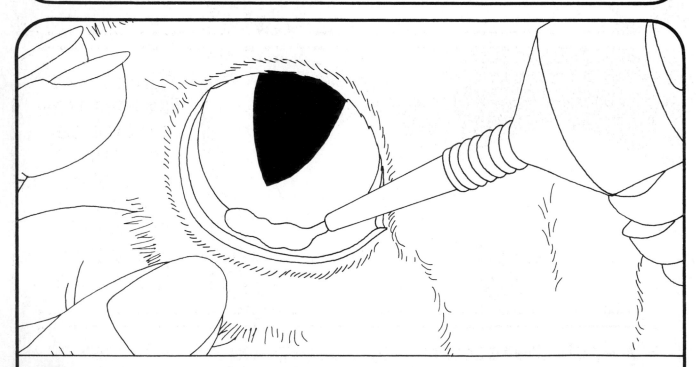

3 Apply the recommended dosage on the lower lid as close to the eye as possible.

APPLYING MEDICINE TO THE NOSE

- **Do not** put medicine in the cat's nose unless your veterinarian recommends it.

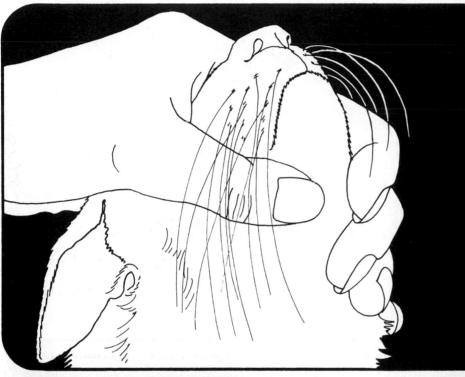

1 **Restrain the cat. See RE-STRAINTS, pages 177-185.** Grasp the cat's muzzle and block its vision with your hand. Elevate the head so the nose points upward.

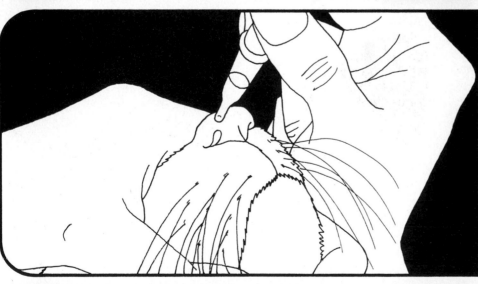

2 Holding the medicine dropper with your fingers, steady the heel of your other hand against the cat's muzzle.

3 Apply the recommended dosage directly into the nostrils. Avoid touching the nose with the medicine dropper.

TAKING THE CAT'S TEMPERATURE

IMPORTANT

- Only use a rectal thermometer.

- Shake the thermometer until it registers below 98°F. (36.7°C.).

- Lubricate it well with petroleum jelly.

- Speak in a gentle, reassuring voice.

- A cat's normal temperature ranges between 99°F. (37.3°C.) and 102.5°F. (39.2°C.); up to 103.5°F. (39.7°C.) if it is excited.

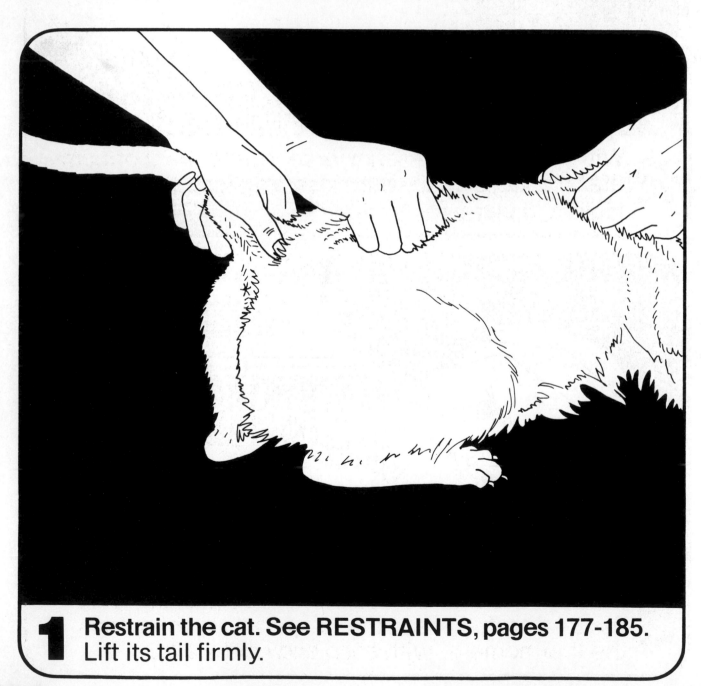

1 **Restrain the cat. See RESTRAINTS, pages 177-185.** Lift its tail firmly.

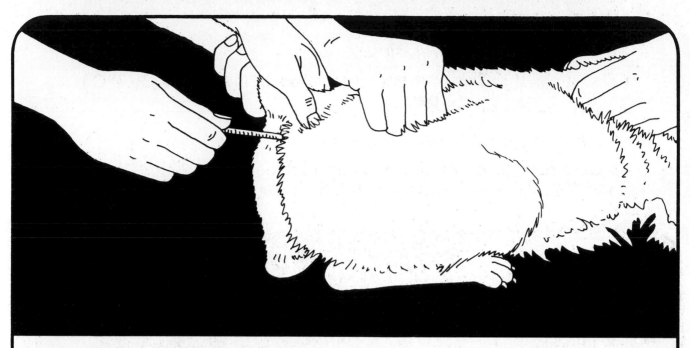

2 Without using excessive force, rotate the thermometer back and forth while inserting it about 1 inch. Hold it in place for 1 minute.

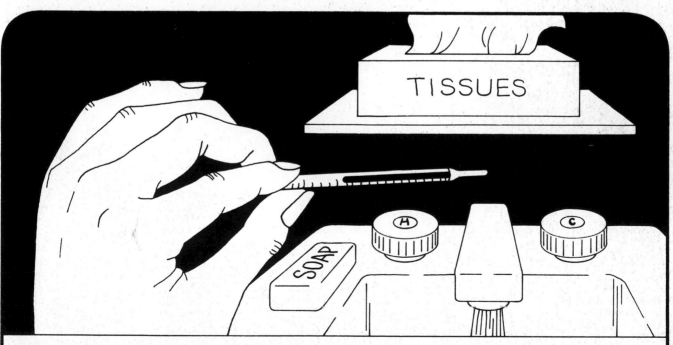

TISSUES

SOAP

3 Remove the thermometer and wipe it clean with a tissue. Carefully read the temperature, then wash the thermometer with soap and cool water.

For our free brochure of health care and first-aid products
for your pet, send your name and address to:

THE
HOME
PET VET
GUIDE

CATS

West Stockbridge, Massachusetts 01266